on **Devising
a Care Plan**

Erica Amende
and Linda Patterson

Published by
**British Association for Adoption & Fostering
(BAAF)**
Saffron House
6–10 Kirby Street
London EC1N 8TS
www.baaf.org.uk

Charity registration 275689 (England and Wales)
and SC039337 (Scotland)

British Library Cataloguing in Publication Data
A catalogue record for this book is available from the British Library

ISBN 978 1 910039 28 1

Project management by Jo Francis, Publications, BAAF
Designed by Helen Joubert Designs
Typeset by Fravashi Aga
Printed in Great Britain by TJ International Ltd
Trade distribution by Turnaround Publisher Services, Unit 3, Olympia
Trading Estate, Coburg Road, London N22 6TZ

BAAF is the leading UK-wide membership organisation for all those
concerned with adoption, fostering and child care issues.

Contents

This series

Ten Top Tips on Making and Writing a Care Plan is the fourteenth title in BAAF's *Ten Top Tips* series. This series tackles some fundamental issues in the area of adoption and fostering with the aim of presenting them in a quick reference format. Previous titles are:

- *Ten Top Tips for Placing Children*, by Hedi Argent
- *Ten Top Tips for Managing Contact*, by Henrietta Bond
- *Ten Top Tips for Finding Families*, by Jennifer Cousins
- *Ten Top Tips for Placing Siblings*, by Hedi Argent
- *Ten Top Tips for Preparing Care Leavers*, by Henrietta Bond
- *Ten Top Tips for Making Introductions*, by Lindsey Dunbar
- *Ten Top Tips for Supporting Kinship Placements*, by Hedi Argent
- *Ten Top Tips for Supporting Adopters*, by Jeanne Kaniuk with Eileen Fursland
- *Ten Top Tips for Identifying Neglect*, by Pat Beesley
- *Ten Top Tips for Making Matches*, by Jennifer Cousins
- *Ten Top Tips for Supporting Education*, by Eileen Fursland with Kate Cairns and Chris Stanway
- *Ten Top Tips on Going to Court*, by Alexandra Conroy Harris
- *Ten Top Tips on Placing Disabled Children*, by Hedi Argent with Robert Marsden

Details are available at www.baaf.org.uk.

Note about the authors

Erica Amende was BAAF's Regional Director in Central and Northern England between 2002 and 2012, following 27 years' experience as a qualified social worker with children and families in the courts and in local authorities. Her work included child protection, care planning for looked after children, youth justice and placing children with foster carers and adoptive parents. She managed a local authority fostering and adoption service for three years, and has chaired adoption and fostering panels. Currently, she acts as a professional adviser for the Independent Review Mechanism.

Linda Patterson qualified as a social worker in 1990 and, since this time, has worked as a social worker in duty and assessment teams and long-term teams, working with children in need, and those subject to child protection plans and care proceedings. She was a Children's Guardian for a number of years, followed by a period working as a practitioner and manager for the NSPCC. Since 2002, she has worked as a local authority manager, initially as a team manager in a long-term team. She has been the service manager for a looked after children and care leavers service for five years, and for the last year, the service manager for a placement, permanence and support service, responsible for the fostering and adoption service and support for all permanent placements for looked after children and young people.

Acknowledgements

We wish to thank all the young people from six Children in Care Councils in England, who travelled from far and wide and generously gave us their time and thoughts, during a consultation day in January 2014. Particular thanks to Scott Deacon and his colleague Ahmed Ahmed, who worked hard to organise the event.

We are grateful to all the social workers and managers in Kirklees Council who offered case examples, read the manuscript at various stages and gave us helpful feedback, including Caroline Money for the "button tree" tool on p 36. Thank you also to the attendees of the first joint Social Work Matters Conference for social workers in Calderdale and Kirklees, which took place in September 2014, for their helpful case examples and tips, particularly Beate Wagner's "Famous Five" in Tip 1.

Special thanks to Priscilla McLoughlin, BAAF Northern Ireland; Sarah Coldrick, BAAF Cymru; and Rhona Pollock, BAAF Scotland, who contributed country-specific legal information. We're also indebted to Sushila de Sousa and Viv Howorth, who scrutinised the draft and helped correct errors. Thanks also to Ahmed Karkhairan and Julie Sunderland for comments on the draft. Any remaining inaccuracies are entirely our responsibility.

Our thanks go to Jo Francis at BAAF for her support and oversight during the production of this book.

Introduction

Care planning is at the heart of everything we do for children who are looked after by local authorities. Good care planning makes the difference between young people reaching adulthood with a settled "secure base" that they have gained during their time in care, and those who have moved many times, have no place that feels like "home", and don't have sufficient resilience or skills to cope alone. A good care plan cannot be written unless much skilled work has been done by social workers and others, so this book is about both writing care plans and the work that underpins them.

History since the middle of the 20th century has taught us four main lessons about things that are damaging for children when care planning. These are:

- drift and delay;
- institutionalised care;
- unnecessary moves;
- failure to incorporate the views of the child.

One longitudinal, detailed study of a large sample of children in care puts the point about drift and delay in no uncertain terms:

> *Overall, the study highlighted that delay in decision-making and action has an unacceptable price in terms of the reduction in children's life chances and the financial costs to the local authority, the emotional and financial burden later placed on adoptive families and future costs to society.*
>
> Selwyn et al, 2006, p 575, quoted in Livingston Smith et al, 2014, p 27

Until the 1970s, it was normal for young children coming into care to be placed in residential nurseries, with babies and toddlers in rows of cots, crying for attention or, worse still, lying there silently. Institutional care for babies and young children was common in the UK and the norm for older children. A study compared the types and sequences of care placements in England and Wales at two points in history: 1980 and 2010. It showed that, in 1980, residential care was the first placement for 46 per cent of children coming into care, whereas in 2010, it accounted for only two per cent. By comparison, foster care accounted for 42 per cent of first placements in 1980, climbing to 75 per cent in 2010. The same study indicated that over the 30-year period, there had been no significant decrease in placement moves, despite various Government strategies (Bullock and Blower, 2013).

Now we understand the crucial importance of one-to-one attention from attuned adult caregivers to a child's emotional and intellectual development, and we express concern about institutionalised child care in other countries. Similarly, in the 1960s and early 1970s, it was normal for children to be in a "one size fits all" placement without much thought for the long term, using a "let's wait and see what happens" approach. Contact with parents or relatives was often stopped or discouraged. The result was that many young people drifted through the system and left care with the worst of both worlds: completely out of touch with their birth family; little experience of family life or close trusting relationships with parent figures; and no connections except for their fellow residents from the children's home. These outcomes were shockingly laid bare in the research study, *Children who Wait* (Rowe and Lambert, 1973). Drift and delay are the worst enemies of good care planning – "let's wait and see what happens" may feel easier than tackling difficult problems, but it is a recipe for long-term failure from the child's point of view.

Permanence planning

It seems strange to us now, but it was only in the 1980s that the concept of "permanence planning" arrived in the UK from the US. It made practitioners think about the whole childhood of children coming into care, and made social workers put themselves in the shoes of a good parent, making plans and taking decisions. If the family problems which had led to the child being looked after by the state could not be resolved to a degree which allowed the child to return home within a reasonable timeframe for him/her, practitioners had to accept their responsibility to plan a settled, secure upbringing (rather than just the child's day-to-day care). The idea of permanence (psychological, physical and legal) has remained key to thinking about care planning, and underlies much of this book. By the end of the 1990s, accumulated statistics about children in care turned the spotlight onto the number of moves they experienced, and highlighted the correlation between numerous moves within care and poor outcomes in adulthood, such as the proportion of formerly looked after children in prison, and their over-representation in the population of adults sectioned under mental health legislation. Trying to reduce the number of unnecessary moves for looked after children remains a challenge for everyone, and has influenced initiatives such as concurrency planning, Fostering for Adoption, and "staying put" schemes for young 18–21-year-olds.

The child's rights and welfare

This brings us on to another of our main points: the child's rights and the paramountcy of the child's welfare. Globally, the UK legal framework is consistent with the UN Convention on the Rights of the Child 1989, which asserts these principles, plus important ones such as listening to the child, and working in partnership with children's parents whilst recognising that sometimes it is necessary to act against parents' wishes if the child is at risk. 1989 also saw a seminal Children Act in England and Wales, written to comply with the UN Convention. It repeated the paramountcy of the child's welfare, and set out key ingredients of care planning, such as parental responsibility; significant harm; the presumption that contact with relatives should be maintained unless it could be shown to be detrimental to the child; and the duty to seek the child's views, those of parents and relatives and anyone else significant to the child before making decisions. It also enshrined the principle of maintaining a child within the birth family wherever possible and safe to do so. Similar legislation followed in other parts of the UK: the Children (Scotland) Act 1995 and the Children (Northern Ireland) Order 1995. A quarter of a century later, these legal foundations for care planning still stand firm. A later legal addition is the Human Rights Act 1998, which brought the UK into line with the European Convention on Human Rights. Relevant aspects for care planning are Article 6: Right to a fair trial, and Article 8: Right to respect for private and family life.

But let us remember that every country has its own laws, meaning that there are differences in the powers given to the state to interfere with parents' rights over their children. These differences affect care planning. For example, in England and the US, adoption means that all the birth parent's legal rights over the child are extinguished, and a looked after child can be adopted even if the birth parent does not consent, providing strict legal requirements are met. But in most European countries, adoption can happen only if the birth parents consent. If they do not, the child remains in foster care or residential care for the rest of their childhood. Consequently, social workers in continental Europe rarely write care plans involving adoption. Most adoptions in Europe are either of relinquished babies, or of children brought in from abroad (intercountry adoption).

A care order in England gives the local authority shared legal parental responsibility over the child: the local authority must consult the parents but has the power to take decisions even if the parents disagree. In some countries, the equivalent of a care order made by a court only gives the local authority the power to care for the child – the parent is still the person who must give consent for all medical, educational and other decisions. This has led to difficulties for children whose parents have long-standing problems and who are unable to exercise this "parental responsibility". For the child or young person, it means that no one is "in charge", and foster carers can feel inhibited from making commitments and plans with them.

DANISH FOSTER CARERS' EXPERIENCES

Half of those interviewed said that they had been told by their social worker not to love the foster child too much...another reflection of the policy that foster carers must not be seen as a replacement for birth parents but as a supplement to them. Even if they manage to give the child love and care and are patient with him or her, it is by no means certain that the child or adolescent will be able to benefit from their efforts...It is paradoxical that whilst studies of relationships between foster families and children show that those who generate emotional attachment to their child get the best results in terms of rates of disruption and continuous support from carers, the official policy up until now has been to discourage this.

Kjeldsen and Kjeldsen, 2010, p 52

Reports and serious case reviews into cases where children have died, or where things have gone badly wrong for children in care, have repeatedly concluded that the child's voice was not heard. Anyone involved with children at risk or in care appreciates only too well that listening to the child, or being able to understand what life is like for the child, is hard. The reality is that in these situations, adults' human rights often collide with children's rights or needs. Children are influenced by those around them and adults may have a vested interest in making sure that outsiders do not find out what the child is experiencing, or how he or she feels about it ("disguised compliance"). Sadly, this may apply to placements within the care system as well as situations before a child is in care.

Exercising "respectful uncertainty", listening to and "learning" each individual child as you develop and write a care plan is a key thread running through the ten top tips in this book. In England and Wales, you will be assisted by the enhanced role of the child's independent reviewing officer (IRO), which requires them to see a child before each review.

Listening to parents, relatives and other people who are important in the child's life makes sense when care planning. Innovative solutions and ideas can arise that practitioners would never have thought of by themselves. Family group conferences have resulted in children being cared for within their extended family network, when it had initially been thought that a lifetime in care would be necessary. One research study (Selwyn et al, 2010) showed that, for black and minority ethnic children, 10 per cent of adoption placements were found through people connected to the child (e.g. school crossing person, teaching assistant, Sunday school helper, child-minder).

We hope that this book encourages you in your work with children and young people. We have provided only the basic details of legal provisions, as these vary from country to country within the UK, so we urge you to check the law, regulations and statutory guidance that apply where you are working. Discuss them with social work and legal colleagues, to ensure that the child for whom you are responsible benefits from accurate consideration of all legal options applicable to his or her individual case.

We hope that we have given you the main points you need to know to help you prepare a robust care plan, and signposted the way to further texts and research studies.

TIP 1

Make your care plan child-specific and meaningful

Whilst this may seems like an easy task, it poses many challenges for social workers. Feedback from young people at a consultation we held for this book in January 2014 would suggest that the quality and significance of their care plans varied enormously.

A research project, entitled *Making Care Orders Work: A study of care plans and their implementation* (Harwin *et al*, 2003), looked at 100 care plans to explore what social workers put in and what they left out, and noted the following:

	Subject	Mentioned in detail	Mentioned briefly	Missed out completely
1.	Child's needs re: their ethnicity, culture, religion, language	1	9	90
2.	Any special education or health needs	72	17	11
3.	How these needs may be met	74	19	7
4.	Aim of the care plan	58	42	0
5.	Timescale	31	20	49
6.	Type or detail of proposed placement	84	16	0
7.	Services by the local authority or other agency	80	17	3
8.	Arrangements for contact or returning home	60	36	4
9.	Support in placement	5	70	25
10.	Likely duration of placement	12	20	68
11.	Contingency plan	28	45	27
12.	Who's responsible for implementing plan	13	50	37
13.	Parents' role in day-to-day arrangements	10	46	44
14.	Wishes and feelings of child, parent/s and others important to child	68	7	25
15.	How child, parents, others will input into decision-making	5	45	50
16.	How disagreements will be dealt with	0	25	75
17.	Arrangements for health care	19	36	45
18.	Arrangements for education	25	37	38
19.	Programme for reviewing the plan	2	47	51

This study was carried out over 10 years ago and some of the omissions in the table are startling. Are social workers doing better now? The young people we consulted told us: 'Care plans should be written in a way so that young people can understand them'; 'Personal information, assumptions and opinions should not be in a care plan'; 'They [young people] need to understand their care plan as not many know about them'; and 'Young people should be allowed to write an introduction about themselves in their care plan'.

Munro, in her 2011 report, noted that:

> *Over half of the children (53%) thought their wishes and feelings didn't usually make, or never made, a difference to the care decisions made about them, while just over a quarter (27%) thought they always or nearly always made a difference.*
>
> *Munro and Department for Education, 2011*

This feedback would suggest that there is still room for improvement.

When does care planning start?

We say it should start when you first begin working with a child and her family, because even if state intervention is short-lived, all your efforts will be towards enabling the child to stay within her birth family, which means thinking about the longer-term sustainability of arrangements alongside reduction of risks and support for the family's strengths.

> *Proactive planning...should begin before a child starts to be looked after, to reduce instances of decisions and placements having to be made in an emergency. This is necessary both to ensure that the most appropriate placement and services are sought*

> *to meet the child's needs, and because it is important that the child, the parents and wider family members (as appropriate), and the carers are clear about the purpose of the period of care...from the beginning of the placement.*
>
> Paragraph 2.26, Care Planning, Placement and Case Review Regulations, Department for Children, Schools and Families (DCSF), 2010

If we only think about the immediate future when we return children home, we risk repeated yo-yoing in and out of care, with resultant harm to children's welfare, referred to as the "revolving door syndrome". Incorporating the long-term as well as the immediate at this stage means that if the child cannot remain within her birth family, the same principles are being applied to alternative care as to the birth family arrangements.

When are written care plans needed?

Care plans are needed for *all* looked after children, whatever their legal route into the care system. In England, a care plan must be prepared within 10 working days of the start of the child's first placement. In care proceedings in England and Wales, an interim care plan is required to be submitted prior to the first hearing, and the court will then set a timetable for the final care plan (Regulation 4(2), Care Planning, Placement and Case Review Regulations (DCSF, 2010)). Once written and shared, the care plan is reviewed regularly, so that if the child or young person's needs change, it can be changed. Statutory guidance also clarifies the differing requirements for children accommodated under s.20 of the Children Act 1989; children who are subject to care proceedings; children where a plan for adoption is being considered; and where the plan relates to the local authority meeting its "corporate parenting" responsibilities.

The Scottish Government states that:

> *Effective and transparent planning procedures for children who become looked after are central to the provision of a service which is fair to all parties; ensures that the aims and purpose of children becoming looked after are carried through; provides stability for children within which their needs and aspirations can be met; operates within timescales which are consistent with children's developmental progress; and can be clearly explained and evidenced to other bodies who have a role in decision making for the child.*
>
> *Scottish Government, 2009, p 20*

What must be in a care plan?

In England, the content of a child's care plan is specified in regulations and statutory guidance (Regulation 5, Care Planning, Placement and Case Review Regulations (DCSF, 2010, and Volume 2 Guidance.) Paragraphs 2.29 and 2.44 of statutory guidance provide very useful information about the areas that should be covered within a care plan and are well worth a read before embarking on the task of writing the plan.

Below is a useful guide to show the different requirements in England, Scotland, Wales and Northern Ireland.

Basis for care plans	England	Northern Ireland	Scotland	Wales
What law/ regulations/ statutory guidance sets out basis for care plans?	Care Planning, Placement and Case Review Regulations 2010, and Amendment Regulations 2013. Children Act Statutory Guidance, Volume 2: Care Planning, Placement and Case Review 2010, and Amendments 2013	Children Order (Northern Ireland) 1995 Guidance and Regulations, Volume 1: *Court orders and other legal issues*; and Volume 3, *Family Placements and Private Fostering Arrangements for the Placement of Children*, Reg 4, 1–3	Looked After Children (Scotland) Regulations 2009, Part II and Schedule 2. Guidance on the Looked After Children (Scotland) Regulations 2009, and the Adoption and Children (Scotland) Act 2007 (published 2011)	Placement of Children's Cases (Wales) Regulations 2007; Review of Children's Cases (Wales) Regulations 2007. Statutory Guidance 2007, *Towards a Stable Life and Brighter Future*
What must be in a care plan?	Long-term plan re: upbringing. Placement plan Health Education Emotional and behavioural development Identity Family and social relations Social presentation Self-care skills Contact arrangements Name of IRO Relevant adults consulted	Child's needs Wishes and views of the child Parental responsibility and capacity Provision of services Type of placement suited to the child's needs Provision for the child's religious persuasion, ethnicity, cultural and linguistic background Contact arrangements Reunification issues Any disability/ special needs Child's development, health and education	Immediate and long-term plan, timescales and steps needed to return the child to their parent or other suitable person. Responsibilities of local authority, persons with parental responsibilities, any carer, responsible manager (if relevant) and child, including role in decision-making on day-to-day basis. Placement details Care needs Health Education Contact arrangements	As per England

What challenges do social workers face in getting this right, and what helps to get there?

As the child's social worker, it can feel like an overwhelming responsibility to prepare a care plan for a looked after child. A good starting point is to acknowledge these feelings, drawing on supervision and peer support, as well as social work theories, research findings and tools to assist you in what can be a daunting task. Be mindful of what you are bringing to this work – your own experiences of being parented and of parenting; your relationships with your immediate and extended family; cultural differences, etc.

It helps to focus on the need to keep the child at the centre of your planning, to refer back to the key principles of child care law, such as:

- avoiding delay for the child by making timely decisions;
- ensuring that the child's welfare is paramount; and
- bearing in mind that children should be brought up in their families, where this is safe and appropriate for the child.

Knowing the child/ren for whom you are planning is also essential through regular visits, relationship building and getting to know the context of the family.

These key principles, combined with your reading of social work theories and research findings, will form the basis of your planning, linked to good assessment and detailed analysis, interlinked with gathering the wishes, feelings and views of the child/young person.

Below is an aide-memoire created for children and families social workers, to help you to keep the most important things in mind when you are in the midst of complex, demanding cases.

THE "FAMOUS FIVE"
Voice of the child: heard, listened to and taken account of – the age of the child is not a barrier
Chronologies and recording: clear and up-to-date, giving a real feel for the child's journey

Management oversight: you are not carrying cases on your own, we take joint responsibility
Supervision: regular, supportive and reflective
SMART plans: specific, measurable, achievable, realistic and time-limited

There is a clear tension between making the care plan relevant, unique and meaningful for the child/young person, and meeting the requirements of care and adoption proceedings and looked after children's review processes. Getting this right requires a degree of creativity and flexibility.

One option is to prepare two care plans: one for court purposes to meet the legislative requirements, and the other, written by the young person themselves, with your help, and which can sit alongside the "formal" care plan, effectively saying the same thing, but in child-friendly language. Many young people we spoke to at our consultation event commented that they found the formal care plan used within social work teams hard to understand. They were not clear what the plan was and what it meant for them on a day-to-day basis. Supporting the young person to make her own care plan in a format that works for her ensures that she will feel part of the process, enables her to add her views in her words, and offers something that is unique to her.

Care plans need to be informed by clear assessments of the child's needs. Recent case law applying to England and Wales (*Re B-S (Children)* [2013] EWCA CIV 1146) requires you to provide the court with a 'global, holistic and multi-faceted evaluation of the child's welfare which takes into account all the negatives and the positives, all the pros and cons, of each option'. This means that you have to evidence a "balance sheet approach", by setting out how you have considered each option available for the child, factoring in what is proportionate, the child's rights under Article 8 to family life, and the paramountcy of the child's welfare for the duration of her childhood.

Brown *et al* (2012) provide a model, entitled *The Anchor Principles: A framework for analytical thinking*, that could assist you to structure your thinking; analyse the information you have gathered as part of your assessment, and pull together a plan that is based on the individual child's needs. It asks you to focus on the following key questions:

- What is the purpose of the assessment that you are conducting?

- What is the child's story?

- What does this story mean for this child?

- What needs to happen for this child?

- How will you know if you are making any difference?

Using models such as this can help you to frame your thoughts, use your professional judgement, consider various hypotheses and, with the assistance of your supervisor within supervision, prepare a care plan that is unique to this child.

Research in Practice's website (www.rip.org.uk) provides some useful online tools to help you to prepare a good, effective care plan. Sinclair *et al* (2007) comment that, 'There is very little that is true of all the children who are looked after by the state'. This highlights the need to personalise each care plan, whilst focusing on key issues. Research in Practice suggests that all plans should cover the following:

- *Provide a sense of permanence for children who cannot live at home with their birth family, supporting the view of the Care Inquiry (2013), which advised that children need security, stability, love and a strong sense of identity and belonging;*

- *Emphasise the overriding importance of relationships in children's lives;*

- *Involve birth families, regardless of whether or not a return home is anticipated;*

- *Include the child's perspective in plans being made for them, posing the following questions – Who is having ongoing conversations with the child to ascertain their wishes and feelings? How is the*

> *meaning of the child's behaviour being understood? Who is trying to imagine how the world looks from the child's perspective?*
>
> Research in Practice, 2014a

One approach recommended by Research in Practice is to adopt a 'framework for thinking based on the linked concepts of "need", "outcome" and "plan". This model 'can help everyone in the child's life work together to formulate, deliver and review plans that start with needs and focus on outcomes' (2014a). For this approach to be effective, it is essential that you have regular reflective supervision and that time is available to build meaningful relationships with children and young people.

What style should I use in writing a care plan?

Statutory guidance in England (DCSF, 2010) states that:

> *Clarity and transparency in the care plan are essential in order so that it can be understood by the child (subject to his/her age and understanding), the child's parents and wider family, the child's carer and a range of professionals who are supporting the child and family.*
>
> Paragraph 2.29, p 18

In the care plan, try to avoid social work or legal jargon and instead use plain everyday vocabulary. Read your draft out loud to yourself: does the meaning you intend come across? Imagine you are the child or her parents: is it clear and does it make sense? Can it be misconstrued? And the most important test: could this care plan be about any child of the same age, or is it really individually tailored for this particular child?

Phrases to avoid include generic statements such as: 'John requires stability and security', or 'Aysha requires carers who can meet her long-term needs'. Statements regarding a child's needs should be specific to the child and show how the plan you are proposing will meet these needs.

Below is a good practice example with regard to a child's emotional needs and contact plans.

> *Settled into a contact routine, Elaine now understands when she is seeing her birth parents and is supported in placement by the strength of her sibling relationships/emotional warmth from her two brothers. She has a close/strong attachment to her mother and needs to be supported with regard to feelings of loss and separation in line with her age, developmental and attachment needs.*

Keep the child at the centre

We asked a group of social workers from Kirklees and Calderdale Council for their advice on writing care plans. Below is their list.

- Always involve the child and be creative in how you do this/how you present their views.

- Know the child: it's their future you are planning for, be clear about their needs.

- Capture the voice of the child, know the child like they are your child.

- Describe and analyse interactions that babies and toddlers have with their carers.

- Speak to the child, observe the child and think long term in terms of the impact on the child.

- If you have a different view to that of the child, explain the reasons why in an age-appropriate way.

- Don't have a "one size fits all" approach to care planning: a good plan must be based on a good assessment, which needs updating as the child's needs change.

- Spend time building relationships with the child/young person so that they understand what your job is; why they can't live at home; what the plan is; how they feel about what is happening in their lives; and record all of this invaluable information.

Recommended reading

For more information, see Boddy, 2013; Care Inquiry, 2013; Research in Practice, 2014a; and Sinclair *et al*, 2007.

TIP 2

Make individual care plans based on good assessment

Introduction

In order to write and review a looked after child or young person's care plan, it is essential to base it on a detailed, up-to-date and comprehensive assessment. This enables all those involved in planning for a child to understand past events and their significance for the child and his family; to have a sense of how the child has been parented; to understand who is involved in his life – parents, grandparents, aunts, uncles, family friends; to understand how the child sees himself within the family; and to gather the views of all those involved, including professionals. Ensuring that the child's voice is heard in this process is critical to understanding the child's journey and planning for this child's future care and protection.

There is a danger that professionals can fall into the trap of viewing assessment as a one-off piece of work, written up in the form of an assessment report. Each time you see a child in any setting, it will add to your assessment of his presentation and his relationships with his parents, siblings, extended family, peers and professionals; it is also an opportunity to gather his wishes and feelings to inform your assessment.

Each assessment, whether as part of a routine visit to the child at home or in placement, or as part of a planned assessment session, should build on information already gathered about the child and his family. This allows you to consider any changes, positive or negative, in the child's presentation, in the care that he is receiving, and in his wishes and feelings.

Gathering information from professionals, such as health visitors, school nurses, teachers, nursery workers, and contact supervisors, etc, is key to understanding the child and his needs. Workers at school or nursery will build up a picture of the child, including attendance each day; physical and emotional presentation; how the child interacts with his peers; how he responds to structure and boundaries; and his stage of development. Contact supervisors will pick up subtle information about how the child relates to parents or siblings, for example, does the child make overtures to the adult or vice versa?

The value of this information when formulating your care plan should not be underestimated. For pre-school children who may not have the language skills to express their wishes and feelings, such observations can provide you with information that you can consider in the context of the child's history, observations in other settings, and the information shared by parents, carers and family members.

For school-age children, they may feel more at ease talking about their worries and concerns with a member of school staff with whom they have a trusting relationship. As part of your assessment, it is essential to make these links with key professionals; missing out on this information will result in gaps in your assessment that will affect the quality and usefulness of the care plan.

When gathering information from parents and family members, consider carefully the evidence to support their comments about their child. There have been numerous serious case reviews where many professionals appear to have fallen into the trap of relying on self-reporting from parents and family members, without seeking information to either corroborate or refute what they say. Make sure that you include positive as well as negative observations; a balanced picture is required even if the recommendation is removal and non-return. What is written is a reflection of the parties involved and how they feel about themselves, their child and each other.

A good assessment at any stage of a looked after child or young person's time in care should question, challenge and seek to establish if there is evidence to support the statements and observations of parents, carers, extended family and professionals. Jo Cleary, Chair of the College of Social Work (2013), stated in response to the publication of the serious case review into the death of Daniel Pelka, 'Everyone involved in working with children must be unrelenting in their focus on the child and their needs and on making sure that children's voices are heard'. (For more information on serious case reviews, see Brandon *et al*, 2011 and 2012.)

Approaches to assessments and assessment tools

There are numerous tools to use as part of your assessment, whether you are at the point of considering whether a child needs to come into care; during the course of the child's time in care or when planning for independence; considering a placement move; or when considering a significant change in the care plan, such as changing a plan for adoption to one of long-term fostering or placing siblings separately.

A good starting point in England and Wales is the *Framework for Assessment* (2000), which provides the foundation for assessing a child of any age in any placement. Each domain in this framework gives you the opportunity to gather and analyse information that should inform your care plan. In Northern Ireland, consult the UNOCINI (Understanding the Needs of Children in Northern Ireland) assessment model. Scotland uses the GIRFEC (Getting it Right for Every Child) multi-agency, holistic approach, which includes Well-being Indicators, the My World Triangle and a Resilience Matrix (Scottish Government, 2012).

Crucial elements of a care plan are a child's ethnicity, culture, language and religion. Address each of these in your assessment so that you build up an accurate picture of this child/young person – vital when planning the most appropriate type of placement and care. Sadly, research suggests that practitioners need to do better in this area. In *Pathways to Permanence for Black, Asian and Mixed Ethnicity Children* (Selwyn *et al*, 2010), the authors studied in detail social workers' understanding and use of key terms around ethnicity and culture. They found that the relevant sections of the assessment framework were often blank or had so little information that it was impossible to understand the child's ethnic background. Children of mixed ethnicity were commonly referred to as "black" even when the ethnicity of the father was unknown, or when the child had been brought up in an exclusively white family setting. The authors commented that the word "ethnicity" was frequently used interchangeably with the word "culture".

When you are writing a care plan, check what is recorded in assessments and make sure that you understand the child's ethnic background, the cultural traditions he has actually experienced (rather than presumed), the language(s) used by parents and other carers, and the meaning of any religious ceremonies and cultural practices. (See also Thoburn *et al*, 2000; and Selwyn *et al*, 2010.)

When working directly with a child, there are many tools to assist you, including the Three Houses Technique (mentioned in Munro and Department for Education, 2011), and the Three Islands Technique (Cooper, 2011), which help to gain an insight into a child's life without having to rely on question-and-answer interviews, which can be intimidating for some children.

Using board games with children and young people as part of an assessment/review of their care plan is recommended by David Shemmings and colleagues (2011). The authors advise that:

This technique helps develop a trusting relationship with the child because it involves the social worker and the child sharing information instead of just the child having to reveal information. In addition, it gives the child something to focus on while you are talking about difficult topics. It can be used with any child happy to play it with you. A simple version is often good for an initial meeting or for those at earlier stages of development. A more complex version can be devised for follow-up meetings or with more developed children.

When assessing whether siblings should be separated or live together, Lord and Borthwick (2008) provide a useful tool to help you to weigh up the factors that you need to consider, enabling you to consider siblings' attachment styles and to rate these. In addition, *Ten Top Tips for Placing Siblings* (Argent, 2008) provides some useful pointers.

Any assessment – whatever tools are used – needs to be tailored to the child/young person concerned and to the issue that you are assessing; must have a solid foundation in attachment theory; and should consider research findings, statutory guidance and relevant legislation. Being aware of issues such as the likelihood of achieving adoption for children of a particular age and sex; the significance of sibling relationships; the success of placements with kinship carers (relatives or friends); and the findings of studies about young people's experiences in a variety of settings are key to making sense of the information that you gather and reaching a conclusion that matches the needs of the child/young person, taking into account his views. For more information on assessment, see also Burnell *et al*, 2007; Horwath, 2009; and Brown *et al*, 2012.

Understanding attachment theory's link to good quality assessments

Wittmer advises that 'Attachment refers to the special bond and the lasting relationships that young children form with one or more adults', and 'refers specifically to the child's sense of security and safety when in the company of a particular adult' (2011).

Attachment theory is central to any assessment of a child and for children in care; it informs decisions regarding placements for children with their siblings, and the frequency and nature of contact with their parents, siblings and extended families. Making these decisions understandably stretches social workers when planning for children to be placed for adoption, in long-term foster placements, in residential care or with connected persons. Using supervision and peer support shares the responsibility and challenges of this complex area of work.

Cooper (2010), writing in *Community Care*, states that, 'Attachment theory focuses on how children form a bond with their primary caregiver and the influence it has on emotional development, growth into adulthood and parenthood'. In the same article, Patricia Crittenden (cited in Cooper, 2010) writes that, 'Attachment theory is the parent–child process by which a person learns how to respond to the world and how they learn from the world, and a fundamental understanding of attachment theories is one of the most important weapons in any social worker's armoury'.

This is because most of the children for whom you write care plans may not have had a positive experience of attachment. They may have experienced primary caregivers who made them feel frightened or confused by responding coldly, cruelly or very inconsistently. Such behaviours by the very people whom a child should be able to trust place the child in a dilemma. In order to survive, the child has to suppress his natural responses (e.g. to get close to others, express distress when hurt) and learn other attachment behaviours that minimise negative repercussions.

Crittenden highlights the dangers of making assumptions, referring to observations made by professionals involved with Victoria Climbié and Peter Connolly. In both cases, these children were recorded as being "happy and smiling" when seen by professionals. An understanding of attachment theory would have assisted the professionals to question this presentation and consider that 'this is a learned defence mechanism. These children have learned that a smile puts their adult carer at ease and makes the child safer' (Crittenden, cited in Cooper, 2010).

Peter Toolan (2008) highlights what he refers to as the 'painful reality for looked after children', advising that:

Many children in alternative care have to live their lives with several mostly unanswerable and troubling questions, which reside at a deep unconscious level. These include: why did my family relationships fail me so badly? What led adults who were my only recourse in the world to abandon or abuse me and why does it continue to hurt so much? There are further, perhaps more fundamental, questions which help children shape their identity and their sense of self: who am I, will I ever belong anywhere or to anyone, why didn't my parents want me enough, and was I ever meant to exist?

Assessments and contact plans

Loxterkamp (2009) considers the challenges of determining contact plans. He points out that many children in care have suffered harm at the hands of their parents and carers and questions whether ongoing direct and indirect contact has the beneficial impact that is hoped for or whether it perpetuates the harm, adding to the child's emotional disturbance. Edward Timpson MP, in a speech delivered at a BAAF conference in November 2013, highlighted that 70 per cent of those adopted in 2012/13 entered care due to abuse and neglect, compared to 62 per cent of all children in care.

The paragraphs above identify the need for assessment to be informed by attachment theory when you formulate and agree contact plans. Argent (2002), Macaskill (2002), Neil and Howe (2004) and Schofield and Stephenson (2009) consider that the following factors should be considered when determining contact plans:

- What is the benefit for the child both now and in the future – how is this evidenced?

- What are the emotional costs, for the child, the carer and the birth family – how is this evidenced?

- If the child is experiencing a degree of distress, is this appropriate or can it be managed, thinking ahead in terms of the child's long-term interests?

- What capacity do the child's carers, parents and key players have to manage contact plans to ensure that they meet the child's needs?

- The child or young person's identity – having a sense of who we are can assist a child to develop into a well-rounded individual, or will this reactivate for the child previously dysfunctional or damaging relationships with a parent or sibling? Moyers *et al* (2006) found that contact can result in the replaying of 'negative relationships – many young people had unresolved difficulties that were re-enacted during contact' (see also Research in Practice, 2014b).

- The child or young person's attachments – enabling a child to understand why they are in care and why they cannot return home – can assist a child to invest in his placement and in relationships with his carer.

- The impact of loss on the child or young person – ongoing contact with birth family members can assist to minimise the child's feelings of loss and rejection, allowing him to see that a parent or family member remains committed to him, all of which can assist the child to have a positive view of himself and his position within the family. The converse can be that ongoing contact can result in further trauma for a child, or a reliving of past trauma.

- The prevention of "future shocks" for the child – if contact is facilitated, will this prevent the child developing an idealised view of his birth family? If it doesn't, will this result in the child having an unrealistic expectation that he may be able to return home?

Using the themes above can assist in determining the nature and frequency of contact at the point at which the child comes into care, as well as reviewing the contact plan as a child progresses through his time in local authority care. For help in writing well-argued and reasoned justifications for contact in your care plan, see *Planning for Contact in Permanent Placements* (Adams, 2012) and consider Macaskill's (2002) guidance in *Safe Contact: Children in permanent placement and contact with their birth relatives*. Her study of 106 children in adoptive and long-term foster placements provides some very useful tips regarding the use of contact agreements; preparation for adoptive and foster families prior to placements; involving the child in plans and the frequency of contact; and recognising that what you agree when the child is aged two will not fit with what is best for a child aged 10. For more information on contact, see also Neil *et al*, 2011, 2013; and Schofield and Simmonds, 2011.

When reviewing care plans, it is important to consider the outcome of previous assessments, whilst also identifying what has changed for the child/young person. Relying, for example, on an assessment of a child's emotional/therapeutic needs conducted in legal proceedings five years previously when assessing and planning for independence may not be appropriate, as: a) a young person's needs and circumstances will have changed; b) any therapeutic needs may have been addressed; and c) the challenges a young person faces when moving into adulthood will be very different. This is not to say that you should ignore the previous assessment – using it to consider what progress a young person has made, what his current needs are, and as a basis for an updated assessment is appropriate and beneficial for the young person at a different stage in his adolescence.

The challenge of analysing information

Many social workers have told us that they struggle with this aspect of assessments. Research in Practice (2014a) highlights the importance of analysis and provides useful suggestions for writing your care plan and agreeing permanency. Boddy (2013) notes that:

> *Becoming "looked after" is just one aspect of complex identity and experience. There is a need to recognise the diversity and individuality of children who become looked after, and to take account of their characteristics and needs... Permanence depends on securing the right placement for the right child at the right time.*

Whether your care plan is one for adoption, fostering, a return home, or residential care, you can use the tools on offer from Research in Practice (2014a) to focus on key questions when analysing the detailed information that you have gathered. These questions include:

- What option will offer the child a "secure base" where there is a low risk of placement disruption?

- If the plan is long-term fostering, how does the child feel about being with other children in a placement or being the only child?

- If there is a plan for adoption, Neil advises that 'There is a need to understand from the children's point of view what impact adoption makes in terms of their experience of family membership and their sense of personal and family identity' (cited in Boddy, 2013).

- Where the plan is adoption, in light of *Re B-S* (2013) (mentioned in Tip 1), you need to evidence that you have weighed up the pros and cons of all the available options for the child.

- Any analysis of the child's ethnic and cultural needs in the short and long term 'needs to focus on the specific needs of individual children and young people' and 'guard against bias' (Research in Practice, 2014b).

- If the plan is for reunification, you need to satisfy yourself that the child's birth parents have addressed the concerns that led to their child coming into care; that they can sustain this; and that there is sufficient and appropriate support in place. Studies by Farmer and Lutman (2010) and Wade *et al* (2011) highlight that a considerable number of children who returned home experienced significant harm and were re-admitted to care – this statistic was 81 per cent where parents were misusing drugs (Farmer and Lutman, 2010).

Revisiting assessments to update care plans

As with assessments, a child's care plan is not static – it should be regularly reviewed in accordance with statutory guidance and legislation. The value of any review is inextricably linked to:

- professionals', parents' and carers' knowledge and understanding of the child;

- the child's wishes and feelings;

- the appropriateness of the level of care provided to the child in placement;

- the quality of any universal or targeted support offered to meet his identified needs; and

- the success of contact arrangements with his parents, siblings and extended family and friends.

Ongoing assessment of the child through statutory visits to him in placement; through discussions with his carers; through observations of contact with family; through gathering feedback from professionals involved; and through discussions with/observations of the child will make any review of the care plan far more meaningful and specific to the child, and will provide clarity as to where he will be living; who he will see in terms of friends and family; where he will access education, training and employment; and what he can expect from all the key players in his life.

TIP 3

Each child is unique: learn this child

Introduction

It goes without saying that you cannot write a care plan without a detailed knowledge of the child, her experiences, her family and her wishes and feelings. At the consultation event we held in January 2014 with young people from six Children in Care Councils, key messages that came across from the young people included:

- please ask us what we want;

- listen to what we have to say;

- don't make assumptions about us;

- don't assume that what works for one young person will work for another; and

● don't agree a plan with others and then tell us about it.

A great deal of the information you need for your care plan can come from social work chronologies and assessments. These documents need to be kept up-to-date and be comprehensive, with clear analysis, conclusions and recommendations.

Whilst parents, extended family and professionals involved can share invaluable information with you, in order to understand the meaning of the child/young person's experiences from birth, you need to seek her views and observe her in a variety of settings.

Every child is unique – they will respond to experiences in their own way. Thomas *et al* (1999) were told by children that social workers need to 'understand the child...I know they would have to know a lot about the child. To know a lot about them could really help. Spend time with them' (p 140).

Articles 12 and 13 of the UN Convention on the Rights of the Child 'enshrine the child's right to express his or her views in all matters' (Research in Practice, 2014b). As the child's social worker, you will need to ensure that these rights are upheld.

Building trust and confidence

The Care Inquiry (2013) noted that 'relationships should be the lens through which all work with individual children, family members and carers should be viewed'. This inquiry highlighted the vulnerability of looked after children and young people and emphasised the value and significance of the relationship they need to build and sustain with their social worker. It also showed that they value relationships with social workers, foster carers, residential workers and others who:

> *...are always there for them; love, accept and respect them for who they are; are ambitious for them and help them to succeed; stick with them through thick and thin; are willing to go the extra mile and treat them as part of their family, or part*

> *of their life, beyond childhood and into adulthood.*
>
> Care Inquiry, 2013

There are challenges for you as a social worker in building these relationships, as there is a need to talk about sensitive, painful and upsetting events with children and young people as you go through each stage of the care planning process.

Research in Practice (2013, 2014b) highlights the factors that you need to consider when talking to children and young people. These include:

> *...finding regular time to speak to the child alone and recognising that building trust will take time; making sense of the child's view of the situation and being aware of the strategies the child may have developed to deal with problems in the family and maintaining an openness to the child's view.*
>
> Research in Practice, 2014b

There is also the possibility that there will be times when you and the young person you are working with will have a difference of view with regard to whether she can return home, with whom she should have contact, etc. Managing the conflict between the young person's views and what is best for her isn't easy. Thomas (2009, cited in Research in Practice, 2014b) advises that 'where a child's wishes are overridden, the child should be given an explanation of the reasons and acknowledgment of their concerns'.

For more information on communicating with children, see also Dalzell and Chamberlain, 2006; Cossar *et al*, 2011; and Ryan, 2012.

So how do you do this?

If you are care planning for pre-verbal children, observations over a period of time and in different settings are essential if you are to formulate a care plan that takes account of her relationships with her primary carers, extended family and siblings. These observations will help you to understand the nature of the child's attachments, the significance of relationships with extended family, and the nature of sibling relationships.

You need this information to answer the following questions:

● Does this child have a secure attachment to her primary carer?

● Can this child make an attachment to another carer if she cannot live within their family?

● Is there a safe option for care within the extended family?

● Should this child be placed with her siblings, based on the nature of the sibling relationships?

In order to evaluate the child's responses and put these into context for this particular child, you will need a good understanding of attachment theory and child development. This will enable you to distinguish between the child's chronological age and their functional age, which is highly relevant when deciding how to engage the child/young person and how you evaluate the information that you gather.

Use observation checklists

Vera Falberg's (1994) observation checklists are really helpful for children under the age of five and can be used for children prior to coming into care and whilst in care. These also allow you to assess how parents and carers respond to the child.

Key questions that she poses include:

● Does the child respond appropriately to being separated from their parent/carer?

● Does the child respond appropriately to their parent's/carer's return?

● Can the child show emotion?

- Is the child interested in their surroundings?

- Does the child respond to physical closeness and accept comfort?

- Is the child passive or withdrawn?

The information that you gather from using these checklists will enable you to reach conclusions regarding the child's attachment with her primary carer and how secure this is, and draw on this information to assess how the child will respond to the care planning options that you are considering.

Direct work with children and young people carried out as part of your assessment to inform your care plan and to review it is key to getting this right and ensuring that it is child-specific. A variety of approaches can be adopted to gather the information. The approach you use should be informed by your understanding of the child's preferred method of communication; her interests and hobbies; the most appropriate venue to carry out this work; and the timing of this work.

The child's parents and carers can help you in determining some of these factors, as can professionals involved in the child's life. However, for this to work, it is essential that you consult the child/young person. Carrying out direct work with an adolescent after a tough day at school is unlikely to be positive for this young person. Conducting this work at a venue that the child associates with contact visits may impact on her ability to engage in this work. Asking the child/young person what's best for her gives her a sense that she is having a say in plans for her, and young people at our consultation event advised that this goes a long way to encouraging them to engage and open up in this work.

Use a feelings board

Using a "feelings board" is a useful and simple way of building a picture of how the child is feeling on a particular day/about a particular issue, for example, placement, contact, education, etc.

START	Happy	Sad
Happy		Happy
Sad	Happy	Sad

Both you and the child work your way around the board by throwing a dice and moving the requisite number of spaces, and, when you land on the next square, explaining when you last felt "sad" or "happy". As you get to know the child better, you can add more words such as "angry", "tearful", "worried", etc. It is good to ask the child or young person to add words.

The focus of any observations and direct work must be to understand the child's experiences of being parented since birth; what impact this parenting has had on her self-esteem; her sense of who she is and her position in the family; who she has significant relationships with – aunts, uncles, siblings, grandparents, family friends, etc – and how resilient she is in light of these experiences and relationships.

When reviewing the child/young person's care plan, you should revisit this information, involving the child/young person in this to check that the information is still valid and relevant. Remember that as children grow up, their understanding of their experiences at home will alter, their relationships will grow and develop, and their sense of who they are will change. Having a sense of a child/young person's hobbies and interests is one way to engage in direct work. Playing football, taking a child swimming, doing crafts, etc, can facilitate discussions about their wishes and feelings, experiences and fears. Being engaged in an activity can take the pressure off the child/young person, who may be reluctant or ill at ease in another setting. The purpose of learning about her interests and talents is so that you can build them into her care plan. They are a crucial part of finding a compatible placement and building the child's self-esteem. When planning this work, give consideration to the needs of children who may have learning difficulties/disabilities or who have differing ways/mediums for communication.

Ascertain the child's position in the family

This example was shared with us by a social worker at the Social Work Matters conference in September 2014. The young person had an interest in fishing, and as a way to engage him in discussions about his care plan, his social worker took him fishing. This provided an opportunity to discuss placement options, challenges that had occurred in previous placements, and to clarify his preferences. This information helped to identify the best possible placement for this young person.

Being aware of a looked after child/young person's position in their family is important when embarking on gathering her views to inform the care plan. As the child's social worker, you may have a view that a child has experienced neglect and harm whilst residing at home. For this child, she may have a strong sense of loyalty towards her parents and/or may be feeling anxious about a parent with mental health issues, drug and alcohol misuse issues, etc. Your knowledge of this child and her perception of her position in her family will inform your analysis of her placement needs.

Use a button tree

Using a button tree is a useful way of ascertaining a child's relationship with parents, carers, siblings and extended family. All you need is a large sheet of paper and an assortment of buttons of various shapes and sizes.

Caroline Money, Team Manager in Kirklees Children's Services, delivers training on this tool and suggests the following approach.

- Position yourself so that you are not seen as a threat by the child.

- Before you begin, ask the child if they are OK and if anyone has upset them that day, as this may influence who they place on their button tree.

- Introduce them to the buttons and ask them to pick a button that they think represents them. (You could do a small demonstration first and choose a button for yourself and describe why that button represents you.)

- Ask them to place their button onto the sheet of paper – anywhere they like. At this stage, do not stick the buttons onto the paper. Then ask them to choose a button which represents a family member or friend.

- Ask them to describe why they have chosen that button for that particular person.

- Then ask them to think about how important that person is to them and ask them to place the button on the piece of paper. The closer this person's button is to the child's button, the more important they are to them.

- Go through each of the child's relatives/friends in turn, asking them why they have chosen that particular button and why they have placed them where they have on the sheet. Allow the child/young person to continue placing people on or around their button. Try not to prompt; however, if you would like to seek the child's view on a particular person and they haven't yet mentioned them, you could do this right at the very end. If you do prompt the child, you need to be clear when writing up your findings why you felt the need to prompt.

- At the end of the session, particularly for a child, they may want to stick their buttons onto the paper and take their picture home with them. Where possible, take a photo of the button tree to reflect upon later and also to include in any assessment you may have undertaken or intend to undertake.

It is important to recognise that any conversation with a child can inform your care planning. Driving her to and from school, contact with family members, to activities and health appointments can facilitate an informal discussion. In addition, views shared by the child with her foster carer, key worker in a residential unit, school teacher, contact officer, etc, need to be collated as part of your care planning and can be utilised in your own discussions. Young people at our consultation event highlighted that they will talk to carers and professionals they feel at ease with, at a time of their choosing and when they are ready.

If it is decided that a child cannot live within her birth family and/or with siblings, you should consider through assessment, observations and direct work how the child will respond in another setting. How you assess this will be influenced by the options for the child. If, for example, you are considering placing a child for adoption on her own, questions to consider include:

- Can the child invest in another family?

- Is her connection with a birth relative so significant that the risk of breakdown is high?

- Is her relationship with her siblings so strong that being placed with a sibling whose plan is not adoption (e.g. long-term fostering or a special guardianship order) is more appropriate than pursuing a plan for adoption?

- For a young person who has experienced emotional harm, considerable disruption, changes of carer and neglect, is a family option appropriate?

- For a 16/17-year-old coming into care, consideration needs to be given to a range of options depending on her experiences, reasons for coming into care, her views, preparation for independence, etc.

Once you have gathered the information, you should then analyse it, weigh up the pros and cons of each option, focusing on the short, medium and long-term needs of the child, and come to conclusions about the child's future. This will allow you to prepare your care plan or update an existing care plan.

TIP 4

It's a multidisciplinary effort: involve others

You really need to draw on others to build up a thorough understanding of a child, the meaning to him of his individual experiences and hence what will be the optimum care plan. For babies and very young preverbal children, it is vital to know as much as possible about their behaviour, which gives us clues about their experiences and emotions. Maximise your knowledge by involving other people who have lived with or worked with the child. Put together, all these observations build a picture of the child's expectations of adult caregivers, which is vital to successful implementation of your care plan, whether that involves rehabilitation home or alternative long-term placements. We consulted looked after young people and asked them who had helped them most with their care plan. Of 33 responses, 15 said the adult where they lived (foster carers); 10 said their social worker; five said their Independent Reviewing Officer; and three said someone else (including a sister and a personal adviser).

The child's parents

If you worked with the child's parents before he came into care, you will have observed their interactions with the child as part of your assessment of their parenting skills and capacity to keep the child safe. You may have been privileged to see some very positive, individual moments between the child and birth parents, which should be shared and recorded.

If you were not involved at this stage, take time to speak to those who did this work. Speak to the child's parents and encourage them to think about their parenting style. This may be very difficult if the situation is adversarial, but it may be the beginning of change: either in a direction that will enable the child to return home; or towards them being a significant adult rather than a full-time parent.

The child's relatives

Relatives may feel that they are in a position of divided loyalties and be reluctant to comment about the child's experiences in his birth family, for fear of undermining parents' efforts towards rehabilitation. However, if you can obtain information from them about how the child behaved in their presence, it may add depth to your understanding of the child. Also, of course, if it is not safe for a child to return to their parents' care, relatives are often a viable alternative.

The child's current carers

Ask the current carers how the child behaved at first. Did they record their impressions of him during the first two or three days? How has that changed? Pay attention to food, bathing, going to sleep, sleep pattern, the child's reactions to the carer's presence and temporary absence. Does the child attract the carer's attention, and if so, how?

What happens when the child is hurt or anxious – does he seek comfort, and how? How does the child react to change or to routines? Ask the carer to note how the child is before and after contact. If siblings are placed together, what are the carer's observations of how the children relate to each other?

CASE STUDY: Simon (part 1)

Simon's mother had learning difficulties and mental health problems caused by drug misuse. She was helped to care for Simon from birth by a daily rota of helpers, without whom she could not have maintained any routine. She found parenting very hard and resisted attending to Simon until he was vociferous. The helpers, on the other hand, were very attentive. By the time he was aged three, Simon had learned how to frustrate and outwit his mother, and normal "toddler tantrums" became enormous battles, with his mother losing control and injuring Simon badly. When Simon came into care, his foster carer noted that he didn't attract her attention and couldn't predict her dependable responses. He sought attention from all visitors to the foster home, expecting them to care for him and obey him.

We know that even young children already have very strong internalised "rules" to figure out how their world works. These "rules" have been created by the interactions the child has had with primary caregivers, particularly in the first three years of life. A child who has had an abusive or neglectful experience of being parented will have very different "rules" from a child who has had stable, nurturing care. Research over two years, looking at the relationship between children placed for adoption and their adoptive parents (Kaniuk et al, 2004), showed that these "rules" are resistant to change, so anyone taking on a permanent parenting role needs to understand the individual child's "internal working model" and be prepared to persevere for a long time before new rules are embedded in the child's mind and ways of behaving.

CASE STUDY: Simon (part 2)

Simon's foster carer worked very hard to teach Simon new "rules" for parent–child interactions by responding to his needs and explaining her behaviour towards Simon and the other children in the household. However, when Simon was placed for adoption with a new mum and dad, he reverted to his "old rules", disregarded the adoptive parents and expected his adoptive older brother to be at his beck and call. Because his social worker understood, she had prepared the adopters for this. They and their older son spent a year explicitly helping Simon to learn how his new family "worked" and how he could enjoy being a child in it. The rest of Simon's childhood was settled; he did well at school and is now a skilled adult in the armed forces.

Ask carers to help with observations for your assessment. As the care plan develops, involve carers in talking about the future and preparing the child for moves. If other foster children in the foster family have moved on to permanence, use that real experience to help the child understand. If not, consider whether there are any other children in care in a similar position whom the child has met (e.g. through fostering support groups) whose story you could use. Otherwise, use one of the many books for children with a parallel story – theoretical moves and placements are hard for younger children to understand. Remember to ask foster carers to capture memories and make mementos of special events in the child's life with the foster family. Many foster carers are very talented at creating albums or memory boxes.

Other adults

Talk to adults who have known the child in different contexts, e.g. nursery or children's centre workers, nurses (if the child has had a hospital stay), school staff, community workers, neighbours, and previous foster carers. Remember the child's Independent Reviewing Officer (IRO), especially if you have a system where the IRO follows the child through his "care career". He or she will play an important part in monitoring and shaping the care plan; research on care planning and the role of the Independent Reviewing Officer can be found at www.uea.ac.uk/centre-research-child-family/child-placement. Look for any patterns in the way the child relates to adults. If court proceedings are under way and a court-appointed guardian is involved, make sure you speak to them.

The child's siblings

If the child is one of a sibling group, note information about the different roles the child plays in this group. Within the overarching principle of keeping siblings together where possible, be aware that some sibling relationships forged under conditions of extreme competition for resources (physical or emotional), emotional abuse (e.g. scapegoating, favouritism) or sexual abuse can be damaging and difficult to "reprogramme". If you need to split siblings, use a sibling assessment, such as that in *Together or Apart* (Lord and Borthwick, 2008). See also Tip 2 on assessment. Record the reasons why the decision to separate was made, so that there is an explanation for the child now and in the future about this important decision. Sibling relationships are potentially the longest lasting ones in our lives. If you have to separate siblings, show what efforts were made to maintain contact if appropriate.

Education professionals

Talk to the child's teacher and make sure that you understand the child's school progress compared to other children of the same chronological age. Bear in mind that more than half of children in care have special educational needs. If the child has a specific additional learning need and the school adopts a successful way of communicating with the child, it will be more consistent for him if you and the carer can mirror this.

Read any specialist (e.g. educational psychologist's) reports and educational plans, and talk to authors/teachers and the designated education officer, so that you feel confident about explaining the child's future educational needs to prospective carers. Find out how the child's school has approached any consequences of the child being looked after; sometimes schools make allowances that can have the effect of disguising a child's educational delay. If a child has missed preschool and/or had a high absence rate in primary years, check whether his grasp of educational "foundation blocks" is secure, as it may affect his progress later on. Remember that whatever problems there are, every child has some talents or something they are passionate about. It does not matter if these are not part of the formal curriculum: ask, note, and ensure that these talents or interests are included in care planning and that they are nurtured. If your care plan is for a permanent family, a hobby or talent may be a valuable shared interest that helps to build connections and self-esteem.

CASE STUDY: Tanisha

Tanisha was an energetic nine-year-old of African-Caribbean heritage. She had educational difficulties and had been waiting for a permanent family for a year. When a drama group visited school, Tanisha took a starring role and her teacher recognised a budding talent, as a result of which her foster carer found a suitable drama group via the local theatre. With Tanisha's consent, her family-finding profile was rewritten, highlighting her talent. A newly-approved single Barbadian adopter who was a musician and actress saw the profile. A year later, Tanisha was well settled with her adoptive mother, enjoying life and developing her acting skills, which in turn gave her more confidence at school.

Health professionals

Read medical assessments; talk to the looked after child's designated doctor or nurse to clarify the implications of any health issues for the care plan. If the child is young or was subject to a child protection plan, speak to any health visitor, GP or paediatrician involved at the time to gain a "baseline" of their development then, compared to the present. Check what immunisations the child has had and, if relevant, any preschool health assessment.

Other social care workers

It is likely that several teams or organisations have come into contact with the child and his family in the past. If the records are not available or do not include the information you want, try to contact individual workers. You would be surprised how much useful information and how many relevant memories people can retain. Remember that fostering and adoption social workers and residential workers are sources of information too. If you are care planning for an adolescent, talk to leaving care staff who will have useful knowledge about what the young person will need to move into independence.

Lessons from disruption meetings and child appreciation days

When permanent fostering or adoption placements have broken down, meetings held to pool knowledge and learn what went wrong suggest that usually a combination of factors is involved. The most common factor is issues about the child and their implications for re-parenting, which weren't understood or appreciated at the time of placement. Child appreciation days (held with permanent carers before the placement starts) allow different people who have lived with or known the child to contribute their insights about "what makes this child tick" and highlight "what works".

Supervision

Every case will pose tricky dilemmas and choices, and conflicts between risk and children's wishes. It is vital that you have supervision that enables you to test out your conclusions, look at relevant research evidence, share your doubts and the feelings that will be generated by the life-changing decisions you have to make when care planning.

Summaries of serious care reviews tell us to challenge ourselves as to whether we have got the following aspects right:

- Keeping the child at the centre and not being diverted by parents' needs.

- Ensuring that parents are honestly engaged, not practising "disguised compliance".

- Guarding against over-optimism about the likelihood of change when there is a history of problems.

Key points for your care plan

- List the categories of people involved in formulating the care plan, to show that it is based on multidisciplinary assessment and consultation.

- Include how carers will help prepare the child for any moves of placement, and how they will be enabled to help the child with such a transition.

- Include a succinct summary of the child's educational needs, and what the local authority will be looking for in terms of any new school, specialist assistance, and any advocacy or support new permanent carers will be expected to give.

- If you can, describe the health and any specialist (e.g. psychological) services that will be available in a permanent placement.

- Include the child's talents and interests, and how these will be catered for.

TIP 5

Consider the options: some myths debunked

Myth one: The perfect placement

One of the reasons children wait too long for a permanent placement is the belief that "out there" is a perfect placement that will meet all the child's (and if relevant, their siblings') individual and collective needs. Occasionally a family is found that does "tick all the boxes" for matching criteria, but more often the combination of individual needs, heritage and personality factors means that such perfection is unattainable. Research suggests that the more fixed the social worker's expectations, the longer a child waits.

> *Children's social workers often had little understanding of the adoption process and many were searching for a two-parent family with children who would match the ethnicity of the child. Some children were not adopted because there was little or no promotion and their social worker believed that adopters could not be found.*
>
> *Selwyn et al, 2010, p 3*

If you are planning a permanent placement, do not reject families who don't meet every criterion. Look at all those who meet 80 per cent, and think about the supports that could be built in to meet the other 20 per cent. Of course, you will prioritise some matching factors over others, but be prepared to "think outside the box". Consider families' parenting styles carefully: one that "suits" the child may prove more sustainable than a tightly-matched family with a different style to anything the child has experienced. Where there are unmet needs, honest discussion with the proposed family, and investigation/procurement of support or resources to bridge the gaps, are key to success.

CASE STUDY: Placement with a family member

Billy, Sam, Katie, Lisa and Alfie were removed from their mother's care following significant social care input linked to their mother's mental health, their father's alcohol misuse, and persistent neglect. The children were placed in two separate foster placements pending decisions being made. A family member came forward to care for all five children. Significant concerns were raised as she had had social care involvement in respect of her own children who were now young adults, she lived in a three-bedroomed house and was caring for her daughter who had additional needs.

After a detailed assessment, focusing on her parenting capacity in the short- and long-term, all five children were placed with their relative with a tight and creative support plan.

Myth two: No detriment

There is a strong imperative to believe that becoming looked after will have a "happy ever after" ending for a child. It is not surprising that social workers and others who have to remove children from their birth families due to abuse or neglect experience some feelings of guilt. Consequently, there is an implicit assumption that if children cannot return home safely, they deserve an upbringing in a more socially and materially advantageous family, to compensate for their loss. It is true but rarely recognised that children often cross class barriers via their permanent placements in substitute families, with benefits but also later costs in terms of disjunction from their roots.

Sadly, we do not read newspaper headlines about the majority of children who do grow up in stable foster or adoptive families, do well at school and college, and hold down jobs. However, for a percentage of children, being in care is detrimental, on top of their damaging pre-care experiences. The longitudinal research, *Costs and Outcomes of Non-Infant Adoptions* (Selwyn *et al*, 2006) followed 130 children who had a care plan of adoption in one large local authority. A total of 74 per cent were placed for adoption, of which some did not proceed to an adoption order. By the end of the follow-up period (11 years after the "should be placed for adoption" decision), 26 per cent were in a permanent fostering placement, but a worrying 12 per cent experienced "unstable care careers" that saw them never settle, moving frequently as their placements disrupted and became more long-distance and specialist residential in nature. When this group was compared with the "stable" groups, clear factors emerged. Overall, a child's chances of *not* being adopted increased 1.7-fold for every extra year of age at the time of reception into care.

Stable group	Unstable group
Came into care at younger age (mean 2.6 years)	Most had one or both birth parents who had been sectioned under mental health legislation
Timely decision-making: placed for permanence quicker	Behaviour and relationship with caregiver at age one gave cause for concern

The messages from this research are clear:

1. Delay in care planning is detrimental to children's welfare.

2. If children display worrying behaviour at an early age, it needs addressing with specialist help.

Sometimes you may be care planning for a child or young person where the risks are high and the probability of a successful stable placement is reduced due to absconding, disruption, or the child's dislike of being in care. Often a young person wants to live with a parent, relative or friend deemed unsafe by the local authority, or is not able to commit to a "permanent family". We have to find the least detrimental option.

CASE STUDY: Richard

Richard's birth family had multiple problems, were known to all the local agencies, but kept them at bay. Richard came into care aged 11 and had a series of placements that all disrupted. It was established that he had been scapegoated and abused by his mother's partner, and had spent time with other families nearby. He began absconding from placements, ending up with those families, none of whom were able to offer him "official" care. Eventually Richard "landed" in an emergency foster placement. He was supposed to move on, but refused. After lots of discussion with his foster carer, social worker and independent reviewing officer, it was clear that Richard felt safe, but could not cope with another move,, nor could he commit himself to the placement after so many previous placement breakdowns. Although it was contrary to policy for an "emergency foster carer", it was agreed that Richard could stay as long as he liked. Richard went on to attend college, pass his driving test and stayed with the "emergency" foster carers until he successfully moved into his own flat, aged 18.

Myth three: Plentiful placements

In court and elsewhere, it is accepted that adoption placements are often scarce, especially for particular categories of children, but it is assumed that permanent fostering placements are easily come by. This is not true – finding a suitable fostering placement is just as difficult. In fact, you could say that it is harder than adoption family-finding, because in the UK there are more regional and country-wide mechanisms for finding adoptive families (e.g. the Adoption Registers for England and Wales, the Adoption Regional Information Service (ARIS) in Northern Ireland, Scotland's Adoption Register). These widen the pool of families available at any time, whereas seeking a permanent foster family will often be "in-house", i.e. families already approved by your agency, or people interested in fostering locally who express an interest in a particular child and are assessed with that child in mind. Exceptions to this are the websites and magazines *Be My Parent* and *Children Who Wait*, which feature children across the UK who need adoptive or permanent foster families.

Yet another area for myth-busting is the belief expressed in courts that there is a plentiful supply of specialist "therapeutic fostering" and "therapeutic residential" placements. This is not the case. Local authorities have learned over the years that expensive establishments miles away from a child's origins do not always "come up with the goods" they promise in terms of outcomes, and in addition leave the child or young person "dislocated" and isolated when it is time to move on.

Shockingly, the difference between children who get a permanent placement and those who wait in "short-term foster care" is often the luck of the draw – the social worker(s) allocated to their case. Time and again one sees that what lies behind children's successful permanent placements is determined work by tenacious social workers. They follow up every possible lead, using their initiative and intuition, being proactive and imaginative. They work closely with adoption and fostering colleagues, maximise the use of every family-finding tool available and, as a result, place children without unnecessary delay, so that they can put down roots and thrive in their permanent new home.

CASE STUDY: Sibling placement

A social worker had to remove four children from their mother's care: three boys and one girl, ranging in age from two to 10 years. They had been at home subject to care orders and had never lived apart. Issues causing the removal were significant domestic violence from the mother's partners and fathers of the children, lack of engagement, and emotional harm from witnessing domestic violence and being asked repeatedly to lie about who was living at their home and what they had witnessed.

The children's social worker worked very closely with the family-finder. Despite knowing that sibling placements for four children were very scarce, they wanted a placement that would allow all four to live together, maintain continuity of schools, friendships and after-school activities. They also wanted relatives who could not offer full-time care to be able to offer respite, and the children to be able to see their mother regularly. Detailed profiles of the children as individuals and siblings were prepared, direct work was undertaken with the children and their mother, and visits carried out to three prospective families. A single carer, who was an experienced parent, was identified and a match was agreed. There followed a period of introductions, further work with the children's mother and a detailed package of support, including respite with relatives. This means that each child has individual time with the carer; their mother supports the placement and shares information regularly with the carer; and each child has an appropriate level of contact with their mother and their extended family members.

The effect of social workers' beliefs and actions on children's care plans is also shown in a longitudinal research study looking at the care pathways of 374 children aged under five in Northern Ireland. It too found inexplicable variations between authorities' use of permanent placements, despite the needs and backgrounds of the children being very similar, and asked:

> *If the needs of the children are central to deciding on a long-term placement, and the children across the five Health and Social Care Trusts were very similar in their backgrounds and needs, why were regional variations found in professional decision-making regarding long-term placements for these children?*
>
> McSherry et al, 2013, p 295

It suggested, 'The reasons for the variations stem from the opinions and values of decision-makers regarding the appropriateness of different types of long-term placement'.

Myth four: The detached planner

Textbooks would have us acting as detached dispassionate professionals, unaffected by the emotional and moral challenges posed by care planning. The reality is that we are human. What happens to children affects us deeply; and we find some individual children easier to "read" or to like than others.

When John Smith, aged four, was killed by his prospective adopters in 2000, the serious case review author, Alison Leslie, said of his adoptive placement that social workers should have asked themselves the question: 'If this were my child, would this be good enough?' Her comments provoked and continue to provoke divided reactions. We would contend that we *should* ask this question when we are care planning for children. Answering this question (and discussing your answers with other professionals) will draw out important points that deserve consideration alongside dispassionate assessment evidence.

CASE STUDY: Sarah

Sarah, aged 16, became involved with a man who had a significant history of violence against women. He was also a drug user and used petty crime to fund his drug habit. Sarah became "besotted" with him and, despite her social worker's efforts, she started to spend more and more time away from her residential unit. She would return with bruising, be under the influence of drugs, and look dishevelled.

Her social worker worked tirelessly to engage her, and engage other professionals and to argue for placements where it was hoped she would be safer. In the end, Sarah was made subject to a secure order. Her social worker understandably struggled with this option but focused on, 'If this was my child, what lengths would I go to to keep her safe?' Ultimately, Sarah thanked her social worker for the daily calls and texts, for collecting her when she was ready to return to placements, and for being part of the decision to place her in a secure unit, recognising that she was spiralling out of control and that she needed this to happen.

TIP 6

Know when it's safe enough to go home

Research findings

There is now a body of research about children returning home from care that provides some strong pointers for practice. Below are some of the key studies in this field.

Harwin *et al* (2003) *Making Care Orders Work: A study of care plans and their implementation*

For 21 months after the making of a care order, this study followed 100 children, whose ages ranged from under one year to 15 years, with an average age of 5.7 years at the time of the order. Parental substance misuse (drugs and/or alcohol) was a major factor leading to the making of a care order in 44 per cent of the cases. A plan of rehabilitation home featured as follows:

- As the initial plan when care proceedings started: 39 per cent.

- Care plan submitted at the final hearing and implemented: 22 per cent.

- Children still at home after 21 months: nine per cent.

- Success rate of rehabilitation home care plan 21 months after date of care order: 41 per cent (compared with adoption 57 per cent; residential care 60 per cent; fostering 68 per cent; kinship care 78 per cent).

The finding that rehabilitation home was the least successful type of care plan was a surprise to many. The study questioned why 13 out of 22 children had to be removed from home again, and found:

- children whose mothers misused alcohol were most likely to go home, but the effect of maternal alcohol misuse and neglect on children's welfare was underestimated;

- local authorities overestimated the power of a care order to bring about change in parents;

- local authorities had difficulty exercising their shared parental responsibility with parents, unless there was a high degree of co-operation;

- rehabilitated children of primary school age were thought to be able to seek help if necessary, but were actually very vulnerable.

Successful rehabilitations home happened when parents were determined and co-operative, and there was multi-agency support in place.

Ward *et al* (2006) *Babies and Young Children in Care: Life pathways, decision making and practice*

This research studied 42 babies taken into care under the age of one, who were looked after for at least 12 months. It followed their progress until they were five or six years old and explored the factors that influenced decisions by parents, social workers and courts regarding the children's care plans. It found that social workers made strenuous efforts to enable them to go home, but over half could not be safely rehabilitated. Key points were:

- Very young children whose mothers have entrenched drug or alcohol problems are unlikely to be reunited with them in a realistic timeframe. The timeframes for adults receiving treatment are not the same as for young children needing care. A better outcome was possible if a mother without these problems had separated from a violent partner.

- Putting off a decision *is* a decision. The longer that young children wait, the more likely they are to experience more moves.

Later research (Ward *et al*, 2010) on the same topic followed 47 babies identified as suffering or being at high risk of suffering significant harm, until they were three years old.

- Of the toddlers who remained with their birth families at age three, 43 per cent were deemed to be at continuing risk of significant harm, because parents' situations had not improved or had deteriorated.

- Parents of 57 per cent of the toddlers who remained with their birth families at age three had managed to achieve "good enough care".

All but one of the parents who made sufficient positive changes had done so before their baby was six months old.

Sinclair *et al* (2007) *The Pursuit of Permanence: A study of the English child care system*

This comprehensive study of the whole care system in England, found distinctly different groups of children with differing "care pathways". One strong finding was that the longer a child was in care, the less likely it was that they would return home. Successful returns home usually happened within six months. Of the children who left care within a year, two-thirds returned home. Among those who had been looked after for a year or more, only around five per cent aged 11–15 were likely to leave, and only about one-fifth of these returned home. If the return home failed and young people came back into care, they had very poor chances of being adopted and were highly likely to experience further movement/disruption in care, and to have poor outcomes. Interestingly, local authorities that returned higher proportions of children home had, on average, higher numbers of children with repeat admissions.

Factors for success in cases where the child returned home after less than two years in care were:

- clarity about preconditions that had to be met for rehabilitation;

- a realistic assessment of whether preconditions were met and a contingency plan if they were not;

- the commitment of all key players (child, foster carer, family, social workers), good communication and careful co-ordination between them;

- purposeful, urgent but measured work by social workers to achieve rehabilitation.

Situations where young people had repeated or late attempts at rehabilitation were:

- young person wished to be home, although sometimes with mixed feelings;

- young person worried about their parent(s) whilst in foster care (e.g. re: mental illness, substance misuse).

The home situation was unable to sustain the young person, give them purpose or "push" to complete education, maintain interests/hobbies, have aspirations for adulthood. Domestic violence, drug misuse and challenging behaviour within the family were predictors of failed rehabilitation.

Successful returns home for these cases were where birth parents' situations had changed for the better; there was some continuity for the young person (e.g. school, contact with previous foster carers or residential unit staff), and they had other supports (e.g. sport, youth groups).

Farmer (2009) 'Reunification with birth parents', in Schofield and Simmonds (eds) *The Child Placement Handbook: Research, policy and practice*, pp 83–101

This useful chapter reviews research in the UK and US, highlighting factors that are relevant for UK social work practice. Farmer also refers to her own research (Farmer *et al*, 2008). For two years, this followed 180 children, aged 0–14, in the care of six different local authorities, who were returned home. Key findings from the research are:

- forty-six per cent of children rehabilitated home were maltreated again;

- a close link was found between parental substance misuse and maltreatment after return home;

- a total of 47 per cent of returns broke down over a two-year period;

- previous failed returns were strongly related to later return breakdowns;

- amongst the reasons for breakdown were the following:

  o older age at return;

  o longer periods in care;

  o poor prior planning;

  o negative impact of changes in birth family during child's time in care;

  o insufficient resolution of family problems that led to placement in care.

McSherry *et al* (2013) *Comparing Long-Term Placements for Young Children in Care: The Care Pathways and Outcomes study – Northern Ireland*

This study found that placement of children returned home was less stable than any of the other permanence options explored, and that support was often not available following return home.

Models to help with risk assessment

The Signs of Safety® model was created in Western Australia in the 1990s, and is now used in over 12 countries, including the UK, where it is utilised by 34 local authorities. The model is a solution-focused, organised approach which counterbalances risk with protective factors in the child's daily life. Another framework is the Strengthening Families Model, also originating in child protection. In England and Wales, a Core Assessment is often used when return home is being contemplated. In Northern Ireland, UNOCINI (Understanding the Needs of Children in Northern Ireland) is the standard model. In Scotland, the GIRFEC (Getting It Right for Every Child) assessment and National Practice Model are being implemented in every local authority.

Making a care plan of returning home

In England, the Government has responded to the research quoted above by issuing regulations and statutory guidance, that set out what workers must do before a child is placed at home with parents.

Statutory Guidance, Volume 2, Chapter 3.9 states:

> *The duty to ensure that a placement is the most appropriate way to safeguard and promote the child's welfare applies not only to placements with unrelated carers, but also to those with parents, other persons with parental responsibility and persons in whose favour a residence order had been made before a child became looked after. Abuse or neglect is the primary reason for social work involvement for nearly two-thirds of children looked after by local authorities; research is demonstrating that about half of those returned to birth families are re-abused. Where a child is subject to a care order because of suffering or being likely to suffer significant harm, it will not be consistent with his/her welfare to return home if the factors which led to previous abuse have not been addressed or resolved. Placement decisions must therefore be underpinned by an up-to-date assessment of the child's needs and family circumstances.*
>
> *DCSF, 2010*

In England, Regulations 15–20 of the Care Planning, Placement and Case Review Regulations 2010 specify that a senior "nominated person" in the local authority must make the final decision to allow a child to return to a parent's care. The areas that an assessment must cover are set out in Schedule 3 to these regulations, and include examination of domestic violence, substance misuse, and mental health problems in all members of the household, and information about any adults who visit the home and who will have contact with the child. So, as stated in Tip 2, you need to base your plan on a thorough assessment, whether the child is returning home early in their "care career" or much later on.

In Scotland, the legal system operates differently from those of other UK countries: instead of a "blanket" order being made, if grounds for concern are established, the law allows a tailored package to be put together by a children's hearing to address the individual circumstances of the case. A child may be made subject to a compulsory supervision order (CSO), with proportionate measures attached to guide, treat, protect or care for the child. Parental rights and responsibilities are not affected by this order. Many children in Scotland are subject to a CSO and placed at home with a child protection plan if required. Reviews of children's cases may decide that children should return home if they have been placed elsewhere, and the Scottish system requires that the child's views are integral to such decision-making.

Writing a care plan of returning home

You may be under extreme pressure to allow a child to return home, possibly on a trial basis. Returns home may be considered at an early stage during court proceedings, or later after several years in care, at a child's statutory review. All the above research gives cause for caution, but it also provides you with a clear message about what needs to be covered in your care plan. You need to think about the child returning home *in the same way* as you would think about a permanent placement in care. You don't have a crystal ball, but you must list the risks of harm. What was the harm that brought the child into care? Has this changed? How severe could the harm be in the future; how likely is it to happen? How old is the child, and what are his individual vulnerabilities? What are the benefits and safety factors, and is the return home likely to be sustainable long-term? Your care plan should show how you have considered all the other options and why you have concluded that successful rehabilitation is achievable. The language you use must be clear to the child's parents as well as to any court, so that any conditions that have to be met and changes that have to be made cannot be misunderstood. The plan should not rely on children to "blow the whistle" if conditions at home deteriorate. If the child suffers a major injury, domestic violence, etc, it is easier to make the decision that he needs to be removed from home again. But if there are regular minor incidents of concern, or standards of care at home verge on neglect, it is harder to remove a child again. Consequently, your care plan should include "cumulative harm" as well as one-off significant harm as thresholds that would trigger action. Your care plan will also include the legal basis under which you propose that a child should return home, and the services that will be provided to support the placement. And last but not least, your care plan will need a "Plan B" if things don't go well.

Rehabilitation as a "least detrimental" option for some young people who strongly resist being in care

Despite our best efforts to protect young people, their dislike of being in care, or their identification with their families, can be so strong that they repeatedly go home, or abscond from their care placement, putting themselves at risk in the process. Sometimes the only realistic course of action is to compromise with them, and agree on a return home whilst demonstrating concern for their welfare and offering support. In these situations, key aspects of your care plan should include a working relationship with the child's parent/s or other adults at home; continuity of school/college; and links through previous carers, friends and activities, which can provide a "lifeline". Research by Nelis and Rae (2009) found that adolescents who were securely attached to their peers were significantly less depressed and anxious than those who had few or insecure friendships.

CASE STUDY: Natalie

Natalie was removed into care aged six, due to domestic violence between her parents, who had an on/off relationship. Her father had a history of violence, aggression towards professionals and drug misuse. Her mother had a significant drug habit and allowed unsuitable adults to move in to the home. At 16, Natalie requested a return home, having experienced two breakdowns of placements in a 16-month period. Her father's situation was reassessed. By now he was in full-time employment, no longer used drugs and had moved in with his parents. Whilst never a fan of social workers, he did engage in the assessment, and demonstrated his commitment to Natalie. The assessment concluded that the benefits of the placement outweighed the risks. Natalie returned to his care and he supported her to access higher education.

Key points for your care plan

- Quote research findings about the need to have evidence that parents have made changes before allowing children home. Set out very clearly what has to change and in what timescale before it will be safe enough for a child to go home.

- Weigh up risks and protective factors in a methodical way and write them into your care plan.

- Your risk assessment should be proportionate to the age and vulnerability of the child or young person.

- Try to include strands of continuity that will act as a "bridge" for the child or young person between their time in care and back at home.

- Set out the events/changes to the balance around risk of harm that will trigger a reconsideration of the rehabilitation.

TIP 7

Consider care by relatives and friends

Introduction

From the first day that you become involved with a child or young person, check out with her and her parents who is involved in their lives and whom they can call upon to assist them in the care of the child, should this be needed on a short- or long-term basis. These enquiries will prove invaluable as you start to prepare your care plan for each child.

Having this information available to you from the point of initial contact with a family means that should a child need to be cared for – whether this is for one night or on a long-term basis – you can identify who can assist; who needs to be assessed; who is best placed to offer care based on checks and assessment, and can agree a plan with the family that meets the child's needs, taking into account their wishes and feelings.

A good assessment (whether at the point of initial contact, as part of a child in need or child protection plan or during legal proceedings) should identify family members and friends who have a meaningful relationship with the child, who understand the challenges the family face, and who can work in partnership with the agencies involved with the family. This fits with all the UK countries' individual assessment models and allows you, as the social worker, to gain a full understanding of who is significant to the child and who can meet their needs, should the parent/s find themselves in a position where they cannot care for their child.

Considering friends and family links back to guiding principles within the Children Act 1989 (England and Wales), the Children (Scotland) Act 1995 and the Children Order (Northern Ireland) 1995, which state that, wherever possible, children should be brought up within their families. This has been further emphasised in England in the Care Planning Regulations (2010), and case law over a number of years confirms the court's expectation that, when consideration is given to taking a child into care and/or planning for adoption, all avenues with regard to friends and family are fully explored and assessed to ensure that a child, provided that it is safe and appropriate, can stay within their family network. Within England, case law also dictates that, where the local authority has played any part in facilitating and/or placing the child with a family friend or relative, this child must be viewed as a looked after child.

The UK development of policy and law around kinship care has been influenced by research, including *Looking after the Family* (Aldgate and McIntosh, 2006) in Scotland, which studies kinship care placements and support. In England, Hunt and colleagues' study (2008), *Keeping them in the Family: Children placed in kinship care through care proceedings*, provides us with a useful insight into the positives and challenges of kinship care. This team followed 113 children placed between 1995 and 2001, following them up from 2004 to 2005. The study found that the success of these placements was greater for those who were aged under five, and whilst the level of disrupted placements was higher than that for adoption, it was considerably lower than the disruption rate in long-term foster care. The researchers concluded that placements with family members are an important option that should be promoted. A key message from this study is that the success of these placements is linked to good quality social work assessments prior to placements. Where the assessment had identified that the carer's parenting capacity was good, better outcomes were noted for the child in placement. Where the assessment had highlighted that parenting capacity was poor, the stability and quality of the placement were often poor, impacting on outcomes for children.

Options to consider when drafting and reviewing your care plan

- Set up a family meeting or use the family group conference model. The Family Rights Group has identified such meetings as a good way of engaging all family members and allowing for early identification of potential options within the family to care for a child.

- If a child needs to be placed in care in an emergency situation, there is the option of placing a child with a relative or friend using temporary approval (in England, Regulation 24, Care Planning, Placement and Case Review Regulations 2010). The equivalent in Wales is Regulation 38, Fostering Services (Wales) Regulations 2003, and in Scotland, Regulation 36(1)(c), Looked After Children (Scotland) Regulations 2009. This enables you to place a child with a friend or relative in such situations subject to checks and an assessment, including determining if the relative has played any part in any safeguarding issues that may be the reason why the child needs to be placed in care.

The advantage of this arrangement is that it allows the child to reside with a relative or friend with whom they may have an established relationship, and may allow the child to maintain friendships and continue attending their school, minimising the level of disruption. The disadvantage can be that the approval for this arrangement lasts just six weeks in Wales, 12 weeks in Scotland and 16 weeks in England. In this time period, you need to determine if the child can go home; if this family member or friend should become an approved foster carer (this requires checks, references, medicals, a fostering assessment and presentation to the fostering panel); and/or whether this family member should apply for a more permanent legal order.

This is considerable work to be done by you, as the child's social worker, in a relatively short space of time. And it needs to run alongside you supporting the child in placement, ascertaining their wishes and feelings, and formulating a care plan that reflects the child's wishes and needs, takes account of the outcome of assessments, and reflects the views of parents, carers, the Independent Reviewing Officer and the other professionals involved.

If you, in discussion with your manager, agree that it is appropriate to place a child using this temporary approval, consider what may happen further down the line: for example, there may be a negative fostering assessment; the court may not grant a special guardianship order (England and Wales), residence order (Northern Ireland) or kinship care order (Scotland); checks may highlight safeguarding issues, etc. Such issues may result in a child needing to be moved again and it is important that you factor this into your decision-making. It can be easy in the midst of a crisis to make the decision to place, but if this option does not in the medium and/or long term provide the child with the security and stability she needs, this decision may result in disruption for the child in terms of moving placement, the severing of relationships that were previously significant for her, and changes to school, friendship networks, etc.

In situations where you are considering a placement with family members, consider what practical, financial and emotional support the family member will need to make this placement work.

CASE STUDY: Millie

Millie, aged five, was subject to a child protection plan due to concerns regarding lack of supervision, lack of routines, and poor school attendance associated with her parents' drug and alcohol misuse. The situation escalated, necessitating a decision that Millie needed to be placed in care pending an application to the court for a care order. Her parents put forward an aunt to care for her. This enabled Millie to remain at her school, access local support such as CAMHS and after-school activities, and remain within her local community, minimising the disruption for her. Following negative assessments of her parents, Millie's aunt secured a special guardianship order for Millie at the conclusion of the care proceedings.

If a child needs to come into care in a planned way, family and friends can initially be assessed using a viability assessment. One method to identify who should be assessed/who is best placed to assist is to hold a family meeting or use the family group conference model. Both allow you to agree with the family who is best placed to be assessed, and have the advantage of engaging parents, extended family and friends in making the best possible plan for a child needing short- or long-term care.

CASE STUDY: Tariq

Tariq is aged two and has developmental delay associated with his mother's alcohol misuse in pregnancy. Both parents have mental health difficulties that impact on how they care for themselves and Tariq on a day-to-day basis. Detailed assessments of the parents have concluded that they are unable to provide a safe and stable home for Tariq throughout his childhood. Several family members from both the mother's and father's sides of the family have come forward to say that they wish to care for Tariq. A family meeting was held with all concerned and Tariq's parents (with the support of their advocate), where detailed information was shared regarding Tariq's current and future needs, the role of his parents in terms of ongoing contact, and the outcome of assessments in terms of safeguarding issues. The outcome was that they all agreed that one family member was best placed to be assessed to care for Tariq, and two other family members would make themselves available to support this carer.

A viability assessment allows the assessing social worker to consider what a family member can offer the child; what their relationship is with the child and her parent, and under what basis they may be able to look after the child. This allows the carer to consider the following: Can they meet the needs of the child? Can they keep the child safe? Can they manage the challenges that parents may present? What support may they require to care for the child? This assessment must also consider the wishes and feelings of the child. The timescales for completing this assessment will be determined by each service and, where there are care proceedings, by the court. In Northern Ireland, a viability assessment must be completed within 12 weeks.

At the conclusion of a positive viability assessment, there can be a number of outcomes, including completing a full fostering assessment with the aim to approve the carer as a friends and family foster carer for the child; or an assessment that leads to the making of a child arrangements order or special guardianship order (England and Wales), residence order (Northern Ireland), or kinship care order (Scotland).

Whatever the route to achieving permanency for the child, it is essential that the assessment considers:

- the child's needs, both now and in the longer term;

- the wishes and feelings of the child, recognising that, for younger children, this detail will come from observations of the child with parents, carers and the applicant;

- the strengths and vulnerabilities of the prospective carer, in recognition that they will be taking on the primary caring role for a child within their network;

- how they will manage contact;

- how they will sustain relationships with the child's parents;

- how they will manage financially;

- how they will safeguard the child; and

- how they will manage the many unknowns, for example, uncertainty regarding the child's health, future applications from parents to seek the return of the child to their care, etc.

If the relative or friend is approved as a friends and family foster carer, the child will remain looked after, with an allocated social worker and regular reviews of the care plan carried out by an Independent Reviewing Officer. In this situation, 'the carer will have no legal relationship with or responsibility for the child and ongoing placement will depend on the carer continuing to be approved as a foster carer' (BAAF, 2014, p 5).

In Scotland, under a kinship care order, there is the flexibility to allocate parental responsibilities and rights between parents and carers on a case-by-case basis, depending on individual circumstances. If the outcome is a special guardianship order or child arrangements order (England and Wales), or residence order (Northern Ireland), this will involve the carer sharing parental responsibility with the birth parents and for this arrangement to meet the child's long-term needs. It is essential that the carer is supported to make the transition from being a relative or friend to being the primary carer.

Making this transition will help the carer prioritise the needs of the child, manage contact and demands made by birth parents, and provide the child with a placement that is safe, secure and which prepares them for adulthood. This comes with a number of challenges, including:

- pressure from the child/young person to return home/have more contact with their parents;

- pressure from parents and their network regarding contact;

- criticism from parents regarding the care being provided;

- divided loyalties, given the need to prioritise the needs of the child rather than the needs of the parent;

- managing safeguarding issues;

- managing financial and practical issues;

- dealing with the child's distress, anger, loss, etc.

Child arrangements orders (introduced in England in 2014 to replace residence orders) define the carer as 'the person with whom the child is to live' and 'gives the carer equal responsibility with the child's parent's (BAAF, 2014, p 4). A special guardianship order 'gives the carers overriding parental responsibility for the child and restricts the parents' involvement in the child's day-to-day life' (BAAF, 2014, p 4). By the year ending 31 March 2014, 3,330 children had left care in England following the making of special guardianship orders, so this is now a significant route to permanence in England. If you are not sure whether permanence with relatives would be best under a special guardianship order or adoption, see Tip 9, 'A word about special guardianship versus adoption'.

Children and young people residing with holders of special guardianship or child arrangements orders in England are classed as "children in need" in line with the Department for Education's (DfE) definition, and can be supported via child in need plans, targeted and universal services. Using the child in need process ensures that a child's needs, wishes and feelings are considered and prioritised for the lifetime of the placement, offering them a permanent home within their network and local community; maintaining friendships; enabling them to attend local schools and reach their potential; allowing them to feel part of the family; and to develop a clear sense of who they are and why particular decisions were made for them.

Selwyn et al (2013, cited in BAAF, 2014), in their research into kinship placements, noted that 'over 70 per cent of kinship carers suffer longstanding ill health or disability and up to two-thirds are suffering from depression'. This stark finding highlights the need to consider not only the support needs of the children but also those of the carers.

CASE STUDY: Placement with a family member

Emma, Laura and Tom were all removed from their mother's care due to allegations of sexual abuse against their mother's partner, and a failure to protect on the part of their mother. A maternal aunt and her partner came forward to be assessed as carers for the children. The children all live with the aunt (subject to a special guardianship order), her partner and their adult son. This has allowed the children to remain in the family, to maintain their schools and friendship groups, and to develop a positive sense of identity, feeling part of the family.

This hasn't been without its challenges, as Emma, aged 11, is very loyal to her mother; Tom, aged five, becomes very distressed before and after contact; and the aunt, who previously supported her sister on a weekly basis to care for the children, manage her finances, etc, has had to step away from this role in order to prioritise the children's needs.

Having a tight support plan in place, which takes account of the needs of each child as an individual and the needs of the special guardianship order holders, and is reviewed regularly in line with child in need processes, has meant that the children have felt listened to and supported; the carers have been supported practically, financially and emotionally; and their mother has been assisted to maintain her relationships with her children without undermining the stability, security and sense of belonging that the children have with their aunt and her family.

___

Key points to consider when preparing and reviewing your care plan

- Always consider relatives and friends when a child needs to be placed in care, either as a planned placement or in an emergency. BAAF (2014, p 3) notes that a 'child's identity needs are more likely to be met' in a placement with friends and family; 'the family is likely to have a stronger commitment to the child'; a 'pre-existing relationship' with the prospective carer can assist the child to accept this placement and that they cannot return home; and extended family placements can (where safe and appropriate) help children maintain relationships with their parents, siblings and extended family.

- Make sure that, as part of any assessment process for the child, you gather details of relatives and friends who are significant in the child's life.

- Check out with the child their wishes and feelings about being cared for by relatives, at all stages in the planning and decision-making.

- Always address safeguarding issues as part of your assessments of relatives and friends. BAAF (2014, p 3) poses the questions, 'Is there a carer who can protect the child now and in the future?' and 'Does the carer fully understand and accept the reasons why the child had to be removed from the birth parents, or might they allow the parents to resume care without adequate evidence of change?'

- Be clear about the legal basis on which a child is residing with a family member or friend – BAAF (2014, p 4) advises that 'the legal framework under which a placement with relatives is effected can have practical, particularly financial, implications for the child and carers as well as interfering with the parents' right to family life'.

- At the point of placing the child, particularly in an emergency, consider the longer-term needs and plan for the child. Focusing only on "today's circumstances" can result in children experiencing further disruption in the longer term. BAAF (2014) highlights the need to consider whether the carer can cope with the parents making applications to resume care and to gain additional contact – such applications can cause disruption to the child; can undermine the placement and lead to family placements disrupting.

- Always address support requirements for the child and carer both in the short and long term; doing so will assist to sustain family placements and ensure that the child is kept safe.

TIP 8

Consider fostering

Living with a foster family is the most common experience for children in care in the UK. In England, for the year ending 31 March 2014, 75 per cent of children in care were fostered, the same percentage as in Northern Ireland. In Wales, the figure was 77 per cent. In Scotland, for the year ending 31 July 2013, 35 per cent of looked after children were in foster care or with prospective adopters. [This figure is low because the definition of a looked after child in Scotland includes children with a care plan of living at home with parents under a supervision requirement, and they constitute 30 per cent of all looked after children].

These foster placements fulfil a wide range of purposes: from part-time respite/short break, through emergency, short-term, to long-term/permanent. They include specialist foster placements for:

● parent and child (where both the parent and child are looked after and need assessment or support, both short-term or long-term);

- young people on remand from the criminal court;
- children with disabilities.

In the UK, they also include looked after children's family members or friends who have been approved as foster carers specifically for that child or children (already mentioned in Tip 7). In this chapter, we concentrate on foster placements that offer potential long-term care and a sense of permanence for children.

But first we want to be clear about foster carers' legal position, and its consequences for the fostered child. A foster carer provides complete practical and emotional care, but has no legal rights over the child. The law allows a foster carer to act as necessary in an emergency to protect a child, but he or she cannot make significant decisions. Those decisions will be made by the child's parents/legal guardian or by the local authority, after consulting with the parents/legal guardian, and depending on the child's legal status. This is a difficult tightrope to walk if you are a foster carer trying to parent in an authoritative, confident way. Selwyn and Quinton, in their research comparing foster care and adoption (2004), found that foster carers were very frustrated with a system that gave them responsibility for caring for a child but did not allow them to make decisions that every parent needs to make. Similarly, this is a most frustrating experience if you are a young person wanting permission for a sleepover, your ears piercing, a new haircut, a school trip or a move to a different school.

In response to consistent feedback from children and young people in care, the Government in England issued statutory guidance about delegating responsibility for decision-making to foster carers. Through regulations (Regulation 4 of the Care Planning, Placement and Case Review (England) Regulations 2010, and the Fostering Services (Miscellaneous Amendments) Regulations 2013), they also made it mandatory to include in a child's placement agreement the arrangements for foster carers to be able to make decisions about:

- medical and dental treatment;
- education;
- leisure and home life;
- faith and religious observance;

- use of social media;
- any other matters that those with parental responsibility for the child deem appropriate.

Similar provisions for foster carers are contained in:

- the DHSSPS Circular 01/10, *Guidance on Delegated Authority to Foster Carers in Northern Ireland*;
- the Welsh Assembly Government Practice Guidance 2011, *Fulfilled Lives, Supportive Communities* for foster carers in Wales.

In Scotland, the legal framework is different: parental responsibilities and rights remain with the parent as the "relevant person", unless and until removed by the court, so in Scotland, more fostered children will seek their parents' permission for decisions about their day-to-day lives.

Young people's thoughts about fostering

When we asked young people about a care plan for fostering compared to other placements, they told us:

> *It's better than adoption because you can still see your family.*
>
> *Children will be free from the dramas with their birth family.*
>
> *It gives a stable family environment.*

Long-term outcomes in fostering

If you are considering foster care for a child, how does it compare with other placements in terms of stability? This is a difficult question to answer, both quantitatively and qualitatively. Researchers point out that studies follow up children for varying lengths of time and that there are significant differences in the ages and characteristics of the children involved. The general principle that the younger the child's age when placed, the less likely disruption is to occur, does apply in fostering, but other factors are just as important. Sinclair (2005) concluded that:

> *The outcomes of placements were influenced by children's characteristics and by their wishes. Children with physical impairments stayed longer in their placements. Difficult and disturbed behaviour was the main reason for placement breakdown, with teenage placements particularly likely to disrupt. Children who did not want to be in the placement were more likely to disrupt.*

The studies included in this research overview found that, of fostering placements made when the child was aged 5–11, up to 25 per cent disrupted when followed up for 10 years or more. Placements made when the young person was aged 11–15 had a higher disruption rate: 40 per cent disrupted in the first year, rising to 50 per cent with longer follow-up.

The study *Belonging and Permanence: Outcomes in long-term foster care and adoption* (Biehal et al, 2010) recorded a disruption rate of 28 per cent for long-term foster care, compared with 11 per cent for adoption, in a sample of 374 children followed up for over seven years. However, the children in stable long-term foster placements of more than seven years' duration were qualitatively doing as well as their adopted counterparts. When the researchers interviewed a small proportion of the fostered children and young people, most felt a strong sense of belonging to their foster families and saw their carers as parental figures. Their responses fell into three main groups.

- Those placed with their foster carers in infancy identified almost exclusively with their foster families. They had no direct contact with their birth relatives, and their foster carers linked the children's perceptions to the severity of abuse or rejection they had experienced.

- The second group had fairly unproblematic direct contact with their parents and seemed to reconcile belonging to two families. Their sense of security in their foster family was strong, despite the lack of legal security.

- The third group had direct contact with their parents, which was difficult and troubling, leading to conflicts of loyalty and a less secure sense of belonging to the foster family.

Looking at carers' contributions to placement stability, Sinclair's overview (2005) found that a parenting style that was warm, encouraging, clear in its expectations of children, and authoritative was significant. This was often linked to proactive involvement with foster children's interests and an ability to respond to the child's emotional (rather than chronological) age. A major strand of research was launched in 1997 by Gillian Schofield and Mary Beek: they studied cases in their fostering sample that contained known predictive factors for disruption, but had defied this and were stable, with children making good progress. The resultant Secure Base model of caregiving (Schofield and Beek, 2014) is proving very useful to foster carers, adopters and social workers, and is being applied internationally. Its five caregiving dimensions (availability, sensitivity, acceptance, co-operation and family membership) are linked to five developmental benefits for the child (trust, managing feelings, building self-esteem, feeling effective and belonging). If you are seeking long-term foster carers for a child, using these dimensions should help you.

Which children will be suited to a foster placement as their long-term care plan? Practice wisdom suggests that fostering helps children who:

- cannot live with parents or relatives but have strong links to them, needing regular contact;

- have very strong loyalties and identity ties to their family, meaning that they would struggle to accept being adopted, but nevertheless need care and upbringing by substitute parents within a secure base;

- do not have strong links to their family but are unlikely to be adopted due to characteristics such as significant emotional or behavioural problems, severe disability, family history of mental illness such as schizophrenia, being older (aged 11 or over), or being an unaccompanied asylum-seeker;

- are young people over 10 who do not want substitute parents, but need family-based care rather than the group living experience of residential care.

CASE STUDY: Jake

Jake is aged four. His care plan for adoption was endorsed by the court when he was almost three, with an agreement that contact with his birth mother would be maintained each month until an adoptive placement was identified. Proactive work was done by his social worker to identify an adoptive placement for him, updating his profile, using adoption activity days, updating his Child Permanence Report, etc. After an adoption activity day, one adoptive family expressed an interest in him. His social worker visited Jake to talk to him about the possibility of adoption, and his reaction was, 'I have a mum, why would I need another?' The adoptive family withdrew, and after detailed supervision and a review of his case, Jake's social worker embarked on a piece of direct work with him about his care plan, his relationship with his birth family and his future, focusing on the question, 'Can he commit to a new family?' The conclusion reached was that he was so resistant to the prospect and viewed his birth family so strongly as his *only* family that a plan for adoption was not viable for Jake. This understandably generated a great deal of debate and soul-searching for all involved, but it was agreed that a plan for long-term fostering was now the right plan for him.

As mentioned previously, children and young people who thrive in their foster families usually want to be there and have established a rapport with their carer/s. A consistent message from young people about their care experiences is the wish to have been more involved and consulted about new placements. Children for whom long-term fostering is appropriate are mostly of school age. We have a moral and legal duty to consult them and record their views. Those views may conflict with their needs, so we should discuss this with them and record why we may not always be able to do what they want us to do. As one young person at our consultation event told us: 'You should go to visit new foster carers and sleep over, once you get used to them being around you, before moving in'.

Achieving permanence through fostering

Despite the dominance of adoption in political and media spheres, most looked after children will never be adopted, and will grow up in foster care. If you are care planning for a child who is in a short-term foster placement and cannot return home, there may be pressure to "convert" this to a permanent one. What do you need to ask and know, to be confident that a short-term placement could be successful in the long term? Key areas to explore are:

- the carer's capacity to promote family membership for the child but also accommodate birth family members;

- long-term commitment to supporting contact with birth family members;

- ability to support the child's education up to and beyond age 18;

- likelihood of providing care when the child becomes a young adult at age 18–21.

We mentioned in Tip 5 the myth of "plentiful placements" and how children often wait as long, or longer, for a permanent foster family than those waiting for an adoptive family. If the child you are responsible for needs a long-term foster family, you need to find out how your authority/Trust goes about achieving this.

Kirklees Council in Yorkshire holds a Permanency Planning Meeting before a child's first review to identify their likelihood of needing permanence through fostering or adoption. If it is fostering, the child's needs and profile are developed and potential placements are explored, including prospective carers undergoing assessment. This means that by the time of a final court hearing, a permanent foster placement that can meet the child's needs is often available, and the court can be informed. This reduces delay for children and allows them to move to their permanent family soon after an order is made by the court.

Celebrating a permanent foster placement

Although a permanent foster placement does not have a special legal status, the point at which foster carers commit themselves to bring up a child to adulthood is important. If you are planning permanence through fostering, find out how your authority/Trust marks this, and talk to the foster carers and the child about doing something symbolic and celebratory. Examples of ways to mark the occasion include a foster carer who planted a tree with the child, a family photo, a party, a special object or memento, or ceremony. Statutory guidance in England advises that when a foster placement is made permanent, it is sensible to review the issues that are delegated to the foster carer: a child's sense of permanence may be enhanced through their foster carer being allowed to make more decisions about their life. In Scotland, a permanence order is not legally restricted to adoption, so it can theoretically be used where a child's care plan is long-term fostering.

Fostering as a step to acquiring parental responsibility via adoption or other legal orders

Once upon a time, "fostering with a view to adoption" was an accepted care plan for a child. Many such children were not adopted due to financial factors (fostering allowances would cease or be replaced by much reduced adoption allowances) or resource factors (foster children's status ensured entitlement to health and educational support services). The practice fell out of favour; instead, it was thought that an adoption placement ought to be just that from the outset, so that the child was introduced to the adopters as their new mother or father – their "forever family". Attempts to increase permanence, reduce delay and lessen the number of placement moves for children in care have led to initiatives involving fostering as a step to permanence, for example, concurrency and Fostering for Adoption.

Concurrency projects were set up in several locations in England in the 1990s, following extensive liaison with the courts. They sought out and approved people who were dual-approved as both adopters and foster carers, whose role was to care for young children removed from their birth families due to abuse or neglect, where there was some chance of a return home. The adopters/foster carers were expected to work closely with social workers and birth parents in an intensive assessment process with high levels of contact, with the aim of returning the child home if clear goals were met. However, all involved understood that, if rehabilitation failed, the child would be adopted by the carers. In practice, the rate of rehabilitation was extremely low: most of the children were adopted. Post-adoption contact levels in these projects were higher than in "conventional" adoption placements, probably due to the relationship that was established between adopters and birth parents during the assessment. The main benefit of concurrency projects was the child needing to endure just one move, from birth parent to permanent carer. The main difficulties were legal: it was argued that the schemes were a "back-door" route to adoption and unfairly prejudiced birth parents' chances of success.

Fostering for Adoption was introduced in 2013 in England as a less contentious way of reducing placement moves for very young children, especially new siblings of children already adopted, who could potentially join their siblings' adoptive family. In 2014, a duty was imposed on local authorities to consider this route to permanence for children. It involves a "light-touch" fostering assessment/approval of people already approved to adopt, and a move into the adoptive family under fostering regulations sooner than would happen under adoption arrangements. It may not reduce the number of moves a child experiences. It is too early to assess the success of this scheme for children, although there is some anecdotal evidence emerging about difficulties of using this approach if there is still any possibility of rehabilitation.

Foster carers (whether related to the child, or mainstream "stranger" foster carers) may consider strengthening their foster child's position by acquiring a legal order that gives them parental rights. If you are planning for permanence for the child, you will need to understand and discuss the pros and cons for adults and the child of each option, especially financial and legal, and you will need to talk to the child to be confident that they understand what is proposed and want this to happen. In the year ending 31 March 2014, 1,740 children left the care system in England due to their foster carers obtaining a special guardianship order (also available in Wales). In Northern Ireland, a residence order would be an option. Alternatively, foster carers may wish to adopt, in which case you need to decide whether the local authority will support them. Research suggests that the most contentious cases are those where the child's ethnicity differs from that of the foster carers: sometimes local authorities have opposed the adoption on the grounds that the child's needs cannot be met by a transracial adoption, regardless of how long the child has lived with the foster carers. Contested adoption proceedings in such cases have invariably resulted in the courts making an adoption order, having ruled that the child's attachments to foster carers and their overall welfare (and wishes) outweigh the negatives of transracial placement.

Fostering: post-18 arrangements

One of the biggest differences between young people in care and those living within their own families is the age at which they leave home. Some young people have been desperate to leave care; many have left fostering placements before they were sufficiently mature or equipped with skills for independent living. Others wanted and needed to stay on in foster care beyond their 18th birthday but were not allowed to. Research by Selwyn and Quinton (2004) found that pressure to move children to independence was one of the issues that most preoccupied foster carers. They concluded that legal provisions should be used more flexibly so that foster carers could continue as a safety net for young people after leaving care.

In recent years, there have been strategies to allow young people to remain at their foster carers under schemes such as "Staying Put" (England), "Going the Extra Mile" (Northern Ireland), "When I'm Ready" (Wales) or supported lodgings. In Scotland, parts 10 and 11 of the Children and Young People (Scotland) Act 2014 give a looked after young person the right to remain in care up to the age of 21, and to be assessed to receive aftercare support up to the age of 26. Some local authorities and universities have excellent schemes to help students or apprentices from a care background (both financially and practically). Find out what these are and make sure that the young person and the foster carer know about them before key deadlines for making decisions about their education or career. If the young person for whom you are responsible has special needs, your care planning will include working with adult services to ensure that their eligibility for services is established, and that the transfer to adult services is smooth.

Writing a care plan for long-term fostering: key points

- Show why other options are not appropriate for this child or young person.

- Explain how fostering will help sustain contact with family members that is beneficial to the child, especially with siblings if they have been separated.

- Include whether you will seek a placement that allows for continuity of school, to minimise disruption to the child's education, and any extra support that the foster carers or other services will contribute, to provide extra help with school subjects or upcoming examinations.

- Where a child has specialist medical/health needs, include whether you are seeking a permanent placement that will allow continuity of consultant/hospital services, or what alternative is proposed.

- If your authority/Trust has any ways of specially denoting permanent foster placements, describe how this will help the child feel secure and settled.

TIP 9

Consider adoption

If you are responsible for care planning for a child who cannot return to their birth family and needs an alternative family for life, you need to think through the option of adoption. In the UK, the legal entity of adoption is very marked and distinct from other legal orders. Once a court has made an adoption order:

● The new adopters become the child's legal parents: all parental responsibility and parental rights and duties over the child are completely transferred to them. Legally, it is as if the child had been born to the adopters. The birth parents no longer have any legal power or rights over the child.

● The adopters are the child's parents for life: unlike other permanence options, adoption does not cease when the child becomes an adult.

● It is irrevocable: an adoption order cannot be discharged even if the child or the adoptive parent later want to "separate". (Another order, for example, a care order, could be imposed, but it would neither remove the adoptive parents' status as legal parents, nor reinstate the birth parents' rights and responsibilities).

Once upon a time, adoption was about babies and simultaneously solved two issues: infertile married couples wanting children and unmarried mothers with children facing the stigma of illegitimacy. In the 21st century in the UK, adoption of children from care is about providing secure, permanent relationships for some of society's most vulnerable children. It is more open, more complex, and likely to involve ongoing support after the making of the adoption order.

So how many children are adopted from care? For England, the Government's statistics for years ending 31 March are as follows:

Year	Number of children adopted from care
1998	2,100
1999	2,200
2000	2,700
2001	3,100
2002	2,100
2003	3,400
2004	3,800
2005	3,800
2006	3,700
2007	3,330
2008	3,180
2009	3,330
2010	3,200
2011	3,050
2012	3,470
2013	3,980
2014	5,050

In England, there has been a high level of political and media interest in adoptions from care, so you might be excused for thinking that more children were adopted, but compared to the total number of children in care, it is only a small proportion: 7.3 per cent in 2014. This compares with 6 per cent in Wales; 3.1 per cent in Northern Ireland, and 1.8 per cent in Scotland for the year ending 31 July 2013. There are big variations between authority's/Trusts' levels of adoptions (between 2008–2011 it ranged from1–12 per cent (DfE, 2012, cited in Thomas, 2013)). Interestingly, these differences had nothing to do with the characteristics of the children. The overview, *Adoption for Looked After Children: Messages from research* (Thomas, 2013), noted that differences were the result of local authorities' own practice, policy, culture and organisational structures, plus the influences of local courts and CAFCASS guardians/Guardians ad Litem. For example, one authority would only consider adoption for children under five, whereas another formally considered adoption for all children under 10 requiring permanence. Look at your authority's permanence/adoption policy, and talk through in supervision whether adoption is likely to be an option soon after a child comes into care.

Ages of children adopted from care

Looking at the ages of children adopted from care in England each year since 2009 shows that 70 per cent are under five years old. All research supports the maxim that the younger the child when placed with adoptive parents, the higher the likelihood of success, and the lower the risk of disruption. This fits with a commonsense understanding of what we ask of a child when "transplanting" them into a family of strangers. We would hesitate to transplant a fully-grown tree; we would expect better success from carefully transplanting a sapling. However, 30 per cent of children were adopted at age five or over: some are the eldest in a group of brothers or sisters; others are "singletons"; and some will have been adopted by their long-standing foster carers. Biehal *et al* (2010) found that adoptions of older children by their foster carers were generally very positive: the children actively wanted to be adopted and both parties were committed to each other before the adoption. The researchers commented that this is an important permanence "opportunity" for children whose age when they entered care may have meant that adoption was never previously considered for them. In England, for the year ending 31 March 2014, just under 15 per cent of adoptions from care were by the child's foster carers. Interestingly, in the US, 56 per cent of adoptions from care are by foster carers, due to generous federal and state subsidies, including medical insurance. This results in the mean age at adoption being 6.3 years in the US, compared to 3.8 years in England.

Benefits and outcomes of adoption

> *Research comparing adoption to long-term care supports the following conclusions about adoption:*
>
> - *It offers greater stability*
>
> - *It offers optimal potential for resilience, particularly if it begins when children are younger*
>
> - *It best promotes children's emotional security, sense of belonging and general well-being*
>
> - *It offers children a lifelong family and support to assist them in the transition to adulthood*
>
> *Livingstone Smith et al, 2014, p xii*

How successful is adoption compared to other permanence options? Biehal and colleagues (2010) followed children up for five–eight years and found a lower disruption rate for adoption (11 per cent) than long-term fostering (28 per cent). However, researchers caution that it is difficult to compare adoption outcomes with other placements, due to the different ages of children when placed. Biehal and colleagues found that children in both stable long-term foster placements and adoption had clinically significant scores of emotional and behavioural difficulties and there was little difference in these groups' average scores, so these particular fostered children were doing as well as the adopted children. Children whose fostering and adoption placements disrupted were found to have had high scores of emotional and behavioural difficulties at the start of the study several years earlier, suggesting that this is a predictor of vulnerable placements and signals the need for support and therapeutic help. It echoes findings by Selwyn and colleagues (2006) about children who never achieved a settled permanent placement (see Tip 5).

Taken as a whole, research and practice wisdom points to adoption being an important care plan for children:

- who come into care when very young;

- where there is evidence that birth parents' capacity to parent safely is seriously compromised and is unlikely to change in a timescale that meets the child's needs;

- where other relatives are unable to offer permanent care to an acceptable standard, or there are significant child protection issues or conflicts between them and one/both birth parents;

- where children need a family for life in which they can be legally as well as emotionally secure, and their need for a new start and to belong to a family outweigh their need for continuity with the birth family.

If you are considering adoption for a child, you will need to apply the relevant welfare checklist and demonstrate that the child's needs for a permanent family outweigh her needs for continuity with the birth family, given her particular circumstances and personality. Think about the quality and likelihood of sustainable relationships with birth relatives and siblings before forming your views about contact after adoption.

It is easy to underestimate the power of a sense of permanence and security for children's welfare. If you speak to different social workers who have placed children for adoption and ask them about the changes that they observed in the children during their first year of being with their adoptive families, you will hear startling examples of children growing rapidly through several shoe and clothing sizes; of hair and skin becoming lush and glossy; of confidence, speech and co-ordination flourishing. This can happen even when the children have come from high-quality foster care: it is the result of being "claimed", belonging and feeling safe which liberates energy for physical and psychosocial development.

What children say about adoption

The children and young people at our consultation event in 2014 told us:

> *It gives young children a chance to start over again with a new family and have plenty of protection.*
>
> *It's most suitable when parents can't have them and they're young.*
>
> *It gives you a stable secure home and safe parenting.*

Other children surveyed about being adopted from care said:

> - *Don't leave us too long where we're being harmed.*
>
> - *Speed up adoption: it takes too long.*
>
> - *Give us more information and a say in what happens.*
>
> - *If we can't live with brothers/sisters, make sure we keep in touch.*
>
> - *Moving us around before adoption makes it hard to believe anyone wants us.*
>
> - *Don't push us into adoption if we want to stay fostered.*

> - *The best thing about adoption is joining a real family, feeling good about it and having a positive future.*
>
> - *The worst thing about adoption is leaving our old family.*
>
> *Morgan, 2006*

Adoption against birth parents' wishes

In the UK and some other countries, an adoption order can be made even if the birth parent/s do not agree. In the rest of Europe, this can only happen in exceptional circumstances in a High Court jurisdiction. Not surprisingly, UK courts need to be absolutely convinced that adoption is necessary and right for a child before making such a life-changing, far-reaching order. You and your colleagues must be able to show that you have weighed up the positive and negative consequences of each permanence option open to you, and demonstrate why adoption is the most appropriate for this particular child. Legal case precedents in England in 2013–14 have illustrated the high level of scrutiny required. If a care plan for adoption is contested in England and Wales, you would be setting out this analysis when applying for a placement order, and addressing the welfare checklist set out in the Adoption and Children Act 2002 (see below).

In Scotland, you would be applying for a permanence order with authority for the child to be adopted (POA) under Section 80 of the Adoption and Children (Scotland) Act 2007. The Sheriff Court would need to be satisfied that:

- the "no order" principle is met;
- the child is likely to be placed, or is already placed for adoption; and that
- the grounds for dispensing with parental consent in Section 31 of that Act are proved.

The grounds are: the parent/guardian is dead; the parent/guardian cannot be found or is incapable of giving consent; or the parent/guardian is unable to satisfactorily discharge their parental rights and responsibilities and is likely to continue to do so. As part of making a permanence order, a Scottish court can extinguish the parental responsibilities and rights of the birth parents. Remember that in Scotland, any child aged 12 or over would have to give their consent to an adoption order (s.32, Adoption and Children (Scotland) Act 2007).

In Northern Ireland, you would apply for a freeing order under the Adoption (Northern Ireland) Order 1987. The freeing process in Northern Ireland can be protracted: in 2012/13, the average length of time from last entry to care to adoption was three years and five months.

In England and Wales, the welfare checklist to the Adoption and Children Act 2002 states that, whenever a court or adoption agency is coming to a decision relating to the adoption of a child, it must:

1. Take the child's welfare throughout his or her life as the paramount consideration.

2. Bear in mind that delay in reaching a decision is likely to prejudice the child's welfare.

3. Have regard to: the child's ascertainable wishes and feelings (in the light of the child's age and understanding); the child's particular needs; the likely effect on the child of ceasing to be a member of their birth family and becoming an adopted person; the child's background and characteristics; and any harm that the child has suffered or is at risk of suffering.

4. Have regard to the child's relationship with relatives or other relevant people (e.g. a foster carer) and consider those people's ability and willingness to provide the child with a secure upbringing that meets the child's needs; the likelihood of the relationship continuing and its value to the child; and those people's wishes and feelings.

CASE STUDY: Leo

Leo first became known to social workers when he was two years old. He had lived with his white English mother and they had moved many times, including to several hostels, to escape from her violent partners. His mother had thought that Leo's father was an Iranian refugee, but subsequent DNA tests indicated that he was not the father. Leo's paternity was unclear: his mother named two previous partners, one of Iraqi background and one of Pakistani origin. Neither could be traced. Comprehensive assessment concluded that the mother was unable to give her son adequate physical or emotional care, and could not keep him safe. There were no other relatives who could offer stable, long-term care. Leo was placed in foster care with a care plan of adoption.

Leo was over three years old when he arrived in foster care and unfortunately was "picked on" by his first carers, who found it difficult to relate to him. He became withdrawn and watchful and began to self-harm. He was moved to an experienced foster carer; work was undertaken with him by a psychologist and Leo responded very well. His social worker undertook many sessions with him, explaining through play and stories the idea of a new adoptive family. This was backed up by the foster carer. Leo was keen for his social worker to find him a new family and was able to talk about the kind of family he would like.

Given his age and the fact that he had suffered emotional abuse (some of which related to his ethnicity), an adoptive family was sought that could offer a high level of emotional warmth and attention, deal with his self-harm (as well as possible rejection by him), and handle his unknown ethnicity. The social workers used regional and country-wide linking mechanisms to identify adopters. They were childless and of mixed White British and Italian origins. The adoptive father did not know his maternal grandfather's origins but believed that he came from North Africa. He himself had dark hair and a swarthy complexion. The couple had felt drawn to Leo and a match was taken to the panel alongside a package of support, including sessions with a psychologist to help Leo move to his new family.

Two years on, Leo is a very settled child in his new family. His behaviour is in line with a child of five and he is the apple of his parents' eyes. His adoptive parents worked with the psychologist and social workers to settle Leo in, and are well prepared to answer his questions about his background when Leo asks.

A word about special guardianship versus adoption

One of the reasons for a dip in adoptions from care in England and Wales after 2006 was the introduction of special guardianship. Since its introduction, the numbers of special guardianship orders have increased each year. In the year ending 31 March 2014, 3,330 children left care in England through special guardianship orders, 10.8 per cent of all children ceasing to be looked after. Combined with those adopted and made the subject of a residence or child arrangement order, 10,070 children achieved permanence altogether that year, an impressive 33.1 per cent out of the total children ceasing to be looked after. Special guardianship is an alternative permanence option in England and Wales that does not extinguish the birth parents' rights completely. A special guardianship order gives parental rights and responsibilities to the named special guardian, and the child must live with them. The special guardian makes all the decisions about the child, and if the birth parent disagrees, the special guardian can override them. Unlike adoption, special guardianship ends when the child reaches 18, and it can be revoked. This has been a popular order for relatives, such as grandparents, aunts and uncles, where parents have long-standing problems (for example, substance misuse or mental illness) that prevent them from parenting safely, and where the relatives feel that they have sufficient resilience and emotional robustness to care permanently for the child. In situations of conflict, a special guardianship order gives them the power to do what is best for the child. However, it can be undone, or birth parents can undermine the special guardian by applying to court for revocation. Research by Jim Wade and colleagues (2014) found that special guardianship is predominantly being used for young looked after children to achieve permanence with grandparents, aunts and uncles. They also found that it has not decreased the use of adoption, although there is wide variation between local authorities in its use.

If you are considering permanence with a child's relatives, you need to weigh up whether special guardianship will be strong enough, or whether adoption is more appropriate. Generally, adoption is felt to be too draconian in such cases, and has the disadvantage of "skewing" biological relationships, for example, if a child is adopted by her maternal grandmother, the grandmother legally becomes her mother, and her birth mother legally becomes her sister. However, each case needs careful thought. Cases in the Court of Appeal in England weighing up the merits of special guardianship versus adoption orders in extended family situations have favoured adoption when the following factors were present:

- birth parents' low acceptance of, or negative attitude towards, the special guardian's role;

- a level of conflict between the birth parents and special guardian;

- birth parents had attempted to upset/undermine or re-determine the placement, undermining the child's security;

- the child had special needs or a disability requiring parental responsibility to be exercised beyond age 18 into adulthood;

- the child had a reasonable understanding of the biological relationships vs the legal/parental roles, and their sense of identity was not negatively affected by adoption.

Writing a care plan for adoption: key points

- Set out a "balance sheet" that shows the positives and potential negatives for adoption, and consider each option, including reunification with birth parents, placement with extended family, fostering by non-related carers, and finally adoption, to demonstrate that nothing else will do for this child. If an option involves risk of harm to the child, specify how serious this harm is and how likely it is to occur over time.

- When making points under positive and negative headings, make sure you relate them to this particular child's needs and vulnerabilities, particularly the effect of any harm that they have experienced.

- Show that you are considering the lifelong effects on the child of being separated from birth parents and family. If the plan is for a child to join previously adopted siblings, this may be seen as mitigating against the separation from birth parents.

- Explain how each option provides or does not provide permanent stability, security (i.e. whether it can be undermined by others), committed carers, and a sense of identity. Adoption is the only option that creates a family for life, and it has a lower breakdown rate than other permanence options.

For more information, see BAAF, 2014.

TIP 10

Consider residential care

In the main, the option of living in a residential home is used for children and young people aged 10 and over. Where possible and appropriate, children aged 10 and under are placed in foster care. The exception to this is where children have a range of physical, behavioural, emotional and learning difficulties; in these cases, they may be placed in residential care. Such placements may be made to access appropriate therapeutic intervention; where a child has had a number of placement breakdowns in foster care; and where the child is displaying behaviour that is so challenging and risky that being placed in a family setting has been ruled out. In Scotland, policy and law emphasise that a child's placement should be determined by their needs, so there is less focus on age when considering residential care. Scottish law places great importance on the young person's views and wishes when reaching a decision about placement. A young person in Scotland may be subject to a compulsory supervision order that can specify that they live in a residential placement.

For children with disabilities and complex needs, there can be a range of reasons that lead to them being cared for within a residential setting. This can relate to the challenges faced by their family in managing the day-to-day care within their home, balancing the needs of other children within the family home, facilitating a shared care arrangement and, on occasions, addressing safeguarding concerns.

Government statistics from 2013 show that nine per cent of looked after children in England and Scotland are placed in residential care, four per cent in Wales, and eight per cent in Northern Ireland.

Care planning and residential care

When preparing and reviewing your care plan, be mindful that placements within a residential home can be a positive option for many young people. For some, living within a family setting may be impossible for them, preferring the option of being cared for by a group of staff rather than in a family home with one or two foster carers. For this group of young people, a residential home offers them the security and stability that they crave whilst avoiding what they may perceive as intense relationships with a foster carer acting as their primary carer. The quality and significance of the relationships between young people, their key worker and other staff in a residential home can help a young person to discuss and manage their feelings and emotions; to avail themselves of a range of opportunities in terms of their education, leisure and social activities. This gives them the opportunity to achieve their potential and develop the skills they will need to lead a full and rewarding life as adults: being able to achieve economic independence; maintain relationships; come to terms with past events in theirs and their families' lives; sustain a home; and manage their finances.

As the allocated social worker, before placing a young person in a residential home, look at the home's Statement of Purpose and consider the mix of young people in the unit and what the impact may be on the young person. Asking the staff within the residential home to carry out an impact assessment is a useful approach to consider. Statutory guidance in Scotland recommends preparation of a risk assessment.

Careful and considered matching will assist you to identify the right placement and to plan in advance of any move, preparing the young person, where possible, facilitating introductions and involving key players in the young person's life, such as parents, siblings, teachers and health professionals.

This approach also allows you to take account of the young person's wishes regarding the placement. Involving the young person at an early stage is essential. Whilst this may seem obvious, many of the young people who participated in our consultation event in January 2014 reported that they were not involved in these discussions and felt that decisions were made for them rather than with them. Some children and young people, due to their complex needs and/or their distress, may not be able to participate fully in this process and it is worth considering a range of approaches to engage with them, but also to identify who knows the child well and who can advocate on their behalf.

When placing a young person in a residential home, you may want to ask him to write a "mini profile" of himself to share with the staff group. Young people reported to us that this approach enabled them to influence how they are viewed by carers, particularly for those young people who may have experienced placement changes. Where there have been previous placement disruptions, this suggestion can avoid young people being "branded as a failure", a significant concern for many young people we spoke to. Whilst they recognised that information from their case file would need to be shared, this approach helped them to feel part of the planning for them, along with allowing them to highlight positive aspects of themselves as individuals as well as their likes, dislikes, interests, friendships and worries. For children and young people who have complex needs and/or communication difficulties, this profile can be completed by a family member, friend or advocate acting on their behalf.

Decision-making for children and young people in residential care

A key challenge for young people living in a residential home can be the question of who can make decisions on a day-to-day basis. As part of our consultation event, young people living in residential homes reported that decision-making caused them upset and frustration where simple requests had, from their perspective, to be escalated up to their social worker and his or her manager. They reported that there was often a delay in getting a decision, which meant that they missed out on an event/opportunity.

It is helpful to use the placement planning meeting to agree on who can make decisions for the young person on a day-to-day basis. Parents need to be key players in these discussions, recognising that they hold parental responsibility, balancing this against the age and maturity of the young person. Involving staff in the residential home is also key to this being meaningful for the child/young person.

One way is to encourage and support the young person to come to the meeting with their list of requests so that clear decisions can be made at this point that are recorded as part of the required paperwork. Young people reported to us that simple queries such as who can agree to their hair being cut can become complicated, leaving them feeling frustrated. Young people's circumstances do not remain static so it is essential that these decisions are reviewed during visits to the young person in placement and at statutory reviews. Be honest and open with the young person where agreement is not given to attend an event, visit a friend, etc. Young people reported to us that knowing why agreement wasn't given was far easier to accept than not getting a decision or simply being told "no".

Preparation for independence

For any young person, preparing them for independence is a key responsibility for their parent/carer. It should be no different for a young person who lives in a residential home. Being assisted to prepare meals; to eat healthily; to open a bank account and learn to budget; to consider options at each stage of their education; and being encouraged to access leisure opportunities and maintain friendships are key tasks for the young person's key worker, the allocated social worker, personal adviser, the young person's family and the range of professionals who may be involved in the young person's life.

The young people at our consultation event emphasised their wish to be involved, to be listened to and to be supported by professionals in whom they had trust and confidence. In many cases, this will be their key worker in the home where they reside.

Assisting young people to make choices that are in their best interests can and does make a significance difference to a young person's future in terms of maintaining positive relationships with family and friends; accessing medical care when they need it and having choices with regard to whom they talk to about their health; receiving education and having access to advice and support from professionals with whom they have a relationship; and pursuing hobbies and interests, being clear that they would like their social worker to show an interest in these.

Young people told us that they did not expect their allocated social worker to "wear all of these hats"; they wanted a say in who supports them in making these decisions. Some young people reported that they did not know their social worker well enough to have some of these personal discussions, preferring to talk to their key worker in their residential home.

The challenges of "group living"

Residential care for any young person requires them to live with other young people and this can present a number of challenges, given the age range of young people in the home; the varied reasons why they may be in residential care; and the "pull" from other young people to engage in "risky" behaviour. It is beneficial for all the young people that there are measures in place to support a young person to manage these dynamics, which can have both positive and negative impacts on them.

Impact assessments prior to placement can assist with this, highlighting the reality of "group living" and of sharing living space with other young people. These assessments allow the residential home to tailor their preparations and planning to each individual child/young person and to factor in the impact on the child/young person of emergency and unplanned admissions into the home.

Risk assessments, regularly reviewed and updated, enable the residential home staff to identify the challenges and risks associated with group living, involving the young person in this process so that they are clear as to whom they can turn to for support, and what measures are in place to reduce the risks so that they can keep themselves safe.

Dealing with the competing demands and needs of young people within a home can be a real challenge. Regular communication between the key worker and allocated social worker is crucial, as is supporting the young person to express their views, to access positive opportunities and to maintain attendance at school and/or college so that they do not miss out on reaching their potential.

Engaging family members is also essential so that positive messages can be given to the young person that are consistent with what they hear in the residential home. Young people reported at our consultation event that the tension between listening to what their key worker is saying is best for them, and the views of their parents, siblings and extended family, can be a source of stress and anxiety. They advised that seeing the key players in their lives working together to do the best they can for them can reduce the stress. This can be a challenge in many situations where young people have been placed in care against the wishes of their parents; where young people themselves have requested to be looked after; and where there are differences of views regarding harm experienced by young people whilst they lived at home.

Residential care for disabled children and young people and those with challenging behavioural and emotional issues requires careful planning and regular review. Identifying the right placement; ensuring that appropriate adaptations and equipment are in place; linking in with the appropriate professionals to sustain a child's medical care and educational provision; and working in partnership with parents is essential to support effective care planning.

As the child/young person's social worker, you will play a key role in making this placement a success – working with placement providers to ensure that the mix of young people in placement will not have a negative impact on the child/young person; ensuring continuity of medical care where appropriate; ensuring that relationships with parents and siblings are promoted; and, as the young person approaches adulthood, liaising with adult services to ensure that appropriate assessments are carried out in a timely manner to transfer the care and support package with minimal disruption for the young person.

Transition to adulthood

For those young people aged 15-plus, residential provision must prepare them for the next stage of their lives. This includes supporting young people to manage their finances; to budget on what may be a limited income; teaching them to prepare healthy meals; assisting them to negotiate their way through applying for training courses, jobs, benefits, housing, etc, i.e. modelling the practice that a good parent would adopt if the young person was living at home.

Devising the pathway plan that is required when the young person is aged 16 years and three months provides an opportunity to set out what skills the young person needs to develop, and who needs to support the young person to achieve this, for example, key worker, social worker, personal adviser, careers adviser, etc. It also builds in regular reviews so that the young person's progress can be monitored and obstacles can be addressed quickly, responding to the young person's changing needs, circumstances and views and allowing for him to consider the next stage of his life in terms of where he will live, what support he will need, and what path he will follow regarding employment and education.

The pathway planning process provides a structured opportunity to consider next steps for the young person. With regards to accommodation, there are a range of options to explore with the young person when they are ready to leave their residential unit. These options include supported lodgings provision, supported accommodation, supported tenancies, floating support, and securing their own tenancy through local authority housing provision, housing associations and private landlords.

For disabled young people, the transition from children's to adult services needs to be carefully planned. Starting this process early and involving the young person is essential. Factors to consider include how to prepare the young person for this move; creating and reviewing a bespoke "transition plan" for each young person that allows for regular visits to the new care setting; allowing time to build relationships with the new care team and involving parents, carers and other professionals to ensure continuity of care; providing access to education and health care; and ensuring that the young person has a voice in this process.

A report from the House of Commons Education Committee highlights the challenges. The Committee noted that:

> *Looked after young people face many disadvantages throughout their childhoods, yet too much is expected from them too soon in their transition to adulthood and independence. The troubling and disruptive events that lead to a child or young person becoming looked after have significant and long-lasting effects, not least on their vulnerability as a care leaver, and can leave them less well-prepared to cope with independence. This relative disadvantage is exacerbated by the inconsistent levels of support available to care leavers as they move into adulthood and embark upon more independent living.*
>
> *2014, p 44*

This report and feedback from young people highlight the need for appropriate preparation for young people for independence and agreeing "moving on" plans with them that reflect the reasons why they have come into care; consider what the impact of this has been on their ability to function on a daily basis; take account of their views; and that are based on an up-to-date assessment of need. Feedback from young people in the Children's Rights Director's Report, *After Care* (Morgan, 2012), reported that nearly half of care leavers (49 per cent) stated that they had been prepared badly for independent living.

Review the plan regularly

Considering the feedback above, where a "moving on" plan is agreed, ensure that you build in regular reviews of this plan and the option of the young person returning to their residential placement if this plan doesn't achieve the desired outcome. Whilst this presents challenges in terms of resource issues, it offers a young person in care the same option available to many young people who have been brought up by their parents. This fits with each local authority's duty to accept young people back into their care if their decision to move to semi-independent living, leave care, or decline leaving care services proves to be premature.

Afterword

We develop our sense of identity throughout our life. It changes as we are moulded by our experiences and our place in the world. As we mature, we review our memories and understanding of our upbringing. As adults, we may come to a very different view of what happened, compared to the versions of our life story that we accepted as children. Some people have easy access to parents or relatives, whom they can ask for information. Those who grew up in care often face two problems: either there is no one they can ask for information, or there are extremely conflicting accounts from relatives about why things happened.

Social workers have an important role as historians for children. What we put in official records will be kept for many years. So when we write a care plan, or make a significant change that will have long-term effects for a child, it is important that we record why decisions were made. We are not omniscient or clairvoyant – we can only make decisions based on the evidence we have at the time. Recording things well may turn out to be our special gift for that child many years later, when they are an adult and apply to access their official file. Helping adults to read and digest the information in old records is very humbling. Good records can have a powerful effect: they can dispel long-held misconceptions, or feelings of low self-esteem. They can enable adults to start a new direction in life, or let go of troubling aspects of their past.

So our last piece of advice to you is: Make a good and comprehensive record of decisions.

Bibliography

Adams P (2012) *Planning for Contact in Permanent Placements*, London: BAAF

Aldgate J and McIntosh J (2006) *Looking after the Family: A study of children looked after in kinship care in Scotland*, Edinburgh: Social Work Inspection Agency, available at: www.scotland.gov.uk/Resource/Doc/129074/0030729.pdf

Argent H (ed) (2002) *Staying Connected: Managing contact arrangements in adoption*, London: BAAF

Argent H (2006) *Ten Top Tips for Placing Children*, London: BAAF

Argent H (2008) *Ten Top Tips for Placing Siblings*, London: BAAF

Argent H (2009) *Ten Top Tips for Supporting Kinship Placements*, London: BAAF

BAAF (2014) *Evaluation of Permanence Options for a Child in Care Proceedings in England*, Practice Note 57, London: BAAF

Biehal N, Ellison S, Baker C and Sinclair I (2010) *Belonging and Permanence: Outcomes in long-term foster care and adoption*, London: BAAF

Boddy J (2013) *Understanding Permanence for Looked after Children: A review of research for the Care Enquiry*, London: Care Enquiry

Bond H (2007) *Ten Top Tips for Managing Contact*, London: BAAF

Bond H (2008) *Ten Top Tips for Preparing Care Leavers*, London: BAAF

Brandon M, Sidebotham P, Bailey S and Belderson P (2011) *A Study of Recommendations Arising from Serious Case Reviews 2009–2010* (Research Report DFE-RR157), London: DfE

Brandon M, Sidebotham P, Bailey S, Belderson P, Hawley C, Ellis C and Megson M (2012) *New Learning from Serious Case Reviews: A two-year report for 2009–2011* (Research Report DFE-RR226), London: DfE

Brown L, Moore S and Turney D (2012) *Analysis and Critical Thinking in Assessment*, Dartington: Research in Practice

Bullock R and Blower S (2013) 'Changes in the nature and sequence of placements experienced by children in care 1980–2010', *Adoption & Fostering*, 37:3, pp 268–283

Bunn A (2013) *Signs of Safety® in England: An NSPCC commissioned report on the Signs of Safety model in child protection*, London: NSPCC

Burnell A, Vaughan J and Williams L (2007) *Family Futures Assessment Handbook: Framework for assessing children who have experienced developmental trauma*, London: Family Futures

Care Inquiry (2013) *Making Not Breaking: Building relationships for our most vulnerable children*, London: Nuffield Foundation

Conroy Harris A (2014) *Ten Top Tips on Going to Court*, London: BAAF

Cooper J (2010) 'The importance of attachment theory for children's social workers', *Community Care*, available at: www.community care.co.uk/2010/11/29/the-importance-of-attachment-theory-for-childrens-social-workers/

Cooper J (2011) 'Social work tools for direct work with children: drawing', *Community Care*, available at: www.communitycare.co.uk/2011/11/07/social-work-tools-for-direct-work-with-children-drawing/

Corrigan M and Moore J (2011) *Listening to Children's Wishes and Feelings: A training programme*, London: BAAF

Cossar J, Brandon M and Jordan P (2011) *'Don't make assumptions': Children's and young people's views of the child protection system and messages for change*, London: NCB

Cullen D and Conroy Harris A (2014) *Child Care Law: A summary of the law in England and Wales* (6th edition), London: BAAF

Dalzell R and Chamberlain C (2006) *Communicating with Children: A two-way process*, London: NCB

Department for Children, Schools and Families (2010) *The Children Act 1989 Guidance and Regulations: Volume 2: Care Planning, Placement and Case Review*, London: DCSF

Departments of Health, Education and Employment, and Home Office (2000) *Framework for Assessment of Children in Need and Their Families*, London: Stationery Office

Dickens J, Schofield G, Beckett G, Young J and Philpot G (forthcoming) *Care Planning and the Role of the Independent Reviewing Officer*, available at: www.uea.ac.uk/centre-research-child-family/child-placement

Fahlberg V (1994) *A Child's Journey through Placement*, London: BAAF

Farmer E (2009) 'Reunification with birth parents', in Schofield G and Simmonds J (eds) *The Child Placement Handbook: Research, policy and practice*, London: BAAF, pp 83–101

Farmer E and Lutman E (2010) *Case Management and Outcomes for Neglected Children Returned to their Parents: A five year follow-up study*, DCSF Research Brief DCSF-RB214, London: DCSF

Farmer E, Sturgess W and O'Neill T (2008) *The Reunification of Looked After Children with their Parents: Patterns, interventions and outcomes*, Report to the DCSF, Bristol: School for Policy Studies, Bristol University

Farmer E, Sturgess W, O'Neill T and Wijedasa D (2011) *Achieving Successful Returns from Care: What makes reunification work?*, London: BAAF

Gilligan R (2009) *Promoting Resilience* (2nd edition), London: BAAF

Harwin J, Owen M, Locke R and Forrester D (2003) *Making Care Orders Work: A study of care plans and their implementation*, London: Stationery Office

Horwath J (ed) (2009) *The Child's World: The comprehensive guide to assessing children in need*, London: Jessica Kingsley Publishers

House of Commons Education Committee (2014) *Into Independence, Not Out of Care: 16 plus care options*, Second Report of Session 2014–15, London: House of Commons

Hunt J, Waterhouse S and Lutman E (2008) *Keeping them in the Family: Outcomes for children placed in kinship care through care proceedings*, London: BAAF

Kanuik J, Steele M and Hodges J (2004) 'Research on a longitudinal research project, exploring the development of attachments between older, hard-to-place children and their adopters over the first two years of placement', *Adoption & Fostering*, 28, pp 61–67

Kjeldsen C and Kjeldsen M (2010) 'When family becomes the job: fostering practice in Denmark', *Adoption & Fostering*, 34:1, pp 52–64

Livingston Smith S and Donaldson Adoption Institute Staff (2014) *Facilitating Adoptions from Care: A compendium of effective and promising practices*, London: BAAF

Long M (2013) *Child Care Law: A summary of the law in Northern Ireland*, London: BAAF

Lord J and Borthwick S (2008) *Together or Apart? Assessing brothers and sisters for permanent placement* (2nd edition), London: BAAF

Loxterkamp L (2009) 'Contact and truth: the unfolding predicament in adoption and fostering', *Clinical Child Psychology and Psychiatry*, 14:3, pp 423–435

Macaskill C (2002) *Safe Contact? Children in permanent placements and contact with their birth families*, Lyme Regis: Russell House

McSherry D, Fargas Malet M and Weatherall K (2013) *Comparing Long-Term Placements for Young Children in Care: the Care Pathways and Outcomes Study – Northern Ireland*, London: BAAF

Moore J (2012) *Once upon a Time: Stories and drama to use in direct work with adopted and fostered children*, London: BAAF

Morgan R (2006) *About Adoption: Children's views on being adopted from care – report by the Children's Rights Director for England*, London: OFSTED

Morgan R (2012) *After Care: Young people's views on leaving care – report by the Children's Rights Director for England*, London: OFSTED

Moyers S, Farmer E and Lipscombe J (2006) 'Contact with family members and its impact on adolescents and their foster placements', *British Journal of Social Work*, 36:4, pp 541–559

Munro E and Department for Education (2011) *The Munro Review of Child Protection: Final report: a child-centred system*, London: Stationery Office

Neil E (2004) 'The "Contact after Adoption" study: face-to-face contact', in Neil E and Howe D (eds) *Contact in Adoption and Permanent Foster Care: Research, theory and practice*, London: BAAF

Neil E, Beek M and Ward E (2013) *Contact After Adoption: A follow-up in late adolescence*, Norwich: Centre for Research on Children and Families, University of East Anglia

Neil E, Cossar J, Jones C, Lorgelly P and Young J (2011) *Supporting Direct Contact after Adoption*, London: BAAF

Neil E and Howe D (eds) (2004) *Contact in Adoption and Permanent Foster Care: Research, theory and practice*, London: BAAF

Nellis SM and Rae G (2009) 'Brief report: peer attachment in adolescents', *Journal of Adolescence*, 32:2, pp 443–447

Plumtree A (2005) *Child Care Law: A summary of the law in Scotland* (2nd edition), London: BAAF

Research in Practice (2013) *Communicating Effectively with Children under Five*, Dartington: Research in Practice

Research in Practice (2014a) *Developing Effective Care Plans*, Dartington: Research in Practice

Research in Practice (2014b) *Communicating Effectively with Children and Young People*, Dartington: Research in Practice

Rowe J and Lambert L (1973) *Children who Wait*, London: ABAA

Ryan M (2012) *How to Make Relationships Matter for Looked After Young People: A handbook*, London: NCB

Schofield G and Beek M (2014) *The Secure Base Model: Promoting attachment and resilience in foster care and adoption*, London: BAAF

Schofield G and Simmonds J (eds) (2009) *The Child Placement Handbook: Research, policy and practice*, London: BAAF

Schofield G and Simmonds J (2011) 'Contact for infants subject to care proceedings', *Family Law*, 41, pp 617–622

Schofield G and Stevenson O (2009) 'Contact and relationships between fostered children and their birth families', in Schofield G and Simmonds J (eds) *The Child Placement Handbook: Research, policy and practice*, London: BAAF

Schofield G and Ward E (2008) *Permanence in Foster Care: A study of care planning and practice in England and Wales*, London: BAAF

Scottish Government (2009) *Guidance on Looked After Children (Scotland) Regulations 2009 and the Adoption and Children (Scotland) Act 2007*, Edinburgh: Scottish Government

Scottish Government (2012) *A Guide to Getting it Right for Every Child*, available at: www.scotland.gov.uk/Resource/0045/00458341.pdf

Selwyn J and Quinton D (2004) 'Stability, permanence, outcomes and support: foster care and adoption compared', *Adoption & Fostering*, 28:4, pp 6–15

Selwyn J, Quinton D, Harris P, Wijedasa D, Nawaz S and Wood M (2010) *Pathways to Permanence for Black, Asian and Mixed Ethnicity Children*, London: BAAF

Selwyn J, Sturgess W, Quinton D and Baxter D (2006) *Costs and Outcomes of Non-Infant Adoptions*, London: BAAF

Shemmings D (2011) *Attachment in Children and Young People*, Dartington: Research in Practice

Shemmings D, Shemmings Y, Wilkins D, Febrer Y, Cook A, Feeley F and Denham C (2011) 'Tools social workers can use to talk to children', *Community Care*, available at: www.communitycare.co.uk/tools-social-workers-can-use-to-talk-to-children/

Simmonds J (2004) *Fostering: Attachment* (SCIE Guide 7), London: SCIE

Sinclair I (2005) *Fostering Now: Messages from research*, London: Jessica Kingsley Publishers

Sinclair I, Baker C, Lee J and Gibbs I (2007) *The Pursuit of Permanence: A study of the English child care system*, London: Jessica Kingsley Publishers

Sinclair I, Wilson K and Gibbs I (2004) *Foster Placements: Why they succeed and why they fail*, London: Jessica Kingsley Publishers

Thoburn J, Norford L and Rashid S (2000) *Permanent Family Placement for Children of Minority Ethnic Origin*, London: Jessica Kingsley Publishers

Thomas C (2013) *Adoption for Looked After Children: Messages from research*, London: BAAF

Thomas C and Beckford V with Lowe N and Murch M (1999) *Adopted Children Speaking*, London: BAAF

Toolan P (2008) 'Guide to attachment disorder', *Community Care*, available at: www.communitycare.co.uk/2008/03/05/guide-to-attachment-disorder/

Wade J, Biehal N, Farrelly N and Sinclair I (2011) *Caring for Abused and Neglected Children: Making the right decisions for reunification or long-term care*, London: Jessica Kingsley Publishers

Wade J, Brown J and Richards A (2010) *Special Guardianship in Practice*, London: BAAF

Wade J, Sinclair I and Stuttard L with Simmonds J (2014) *Investigating Special Guardianship: experiences, outcomes and challenges*, DfE Research Briefing DFE-RB372, London: DfE

Ward H, Brown R, Westlake D and Munro E (2010) *Infants Suffering, or Likely to Suffer, Significant Harm: A prospective longitudinal study*, London: DfE

Ward H, Munro ER and Dearden C (2006) *Babies and Young Children in Care: Life pathways, decision making and practice*, London: Jessica Kingsley Publishers

Wittmer D (2011) *Attachment: What works?*, Nashville: Centre on the Social and Emotional Foundations for Early Learning, Vanderbilt University